1992 SUPPLEMENT

to

CASES AND MATERIALS

ON

EMPLOYMENT LAW

SECOND EDITION

By

MARK A. ROTHSTEIN
Law Foundation Professor of Law
University of Houston

ANDRIA S. KNAPP
Visiting Associate Professor of Law
Golden Gate University

LANCE LIEBMAN
Dean and Professor of Law
Columbia University

Westbury, New York
THE FOUNDATION PRESS, INC.
1992

R., K. & L. Cs.Employ.Law 2nd Ed. UCS
1992 Supp.

TABLE OF CONTENTS

PART III. TERMS AND CONDITIONS OF EMPLOYMENT

PART IV. TERMINATING THE RELATIONSHIP

*

TABLE OF CASES

Principal cases are in italic type. Non-principal cases are in roman type. References are to Pages.

TABLE OF CASES

*

1992 SUPPLEMENT

to

CASES AND MATERIALS

ON

EMPLOYMENT LAW

*

Part I

BACKGROUND

Chapter 2

THE DEVELOPMENT OF EMPLOYMENT LAW

A. THE FOUNDATIONS OF EMPLOYMENT LAW

2. EMPLOYER–EMPLOYEE

Page 22. Please add the following to the end of note 2.

Courts have split over whether illegally employed minors, injured or killed on the job, should be limited to workers' compensation. See Fanion v. McNeal, 577 A.2d 2 (Me.1990) (minor, even though employed in violation of child labor laws, was limited to remedies provided by workers' compensation act and was precluded from wrongful death action). Other courts have found this outcome to be unjust and contrary to public policy. See Blancato v. Feldspar Corp., 203 Conn. 34, 522 A.2d 1235 (1987) (child may void an illegal contract and thus may pursue workers' compensation claim or tort action).

Page 22. Please add the following to the end of note 3.

See also S.G. Borello & Sons, Inc. v. Department of Industrial Relations, 48 Cal.3d 341, 256 Cal.Rptr. 543, 769 P.2d 399 (1989) (agricultural laborers are not independent contractors and therefore are eligible for workers' compensation); Northwest Advancement, Inc. v. State, Bureau of Labor, 96 Or.App. 133, 772 P.2d 934 (1989), review denied 308 Or. 315, 779 P.2d 618 (1989), cert. denied 495 U.S. 932 (1990) (minors, employed as door-to-door salespersons, were employees and not independent contractors for purpose of wage and hour regulations).

For a particularly novel attempt to characterize a personal injury suit as falling under a state workers' compensation act, see Houston v. Quincy Post 5129, 188 Ill.App.3d 732, 135 Ill.Dec. 929, 544 N.E.2d 425 (1989) (reversal of trial court's finding that claimant, injured while helping to conduct a bingo game, was employee and not volunteer).

3. EMPLOYMENT AT WILL

Page 28. Please add the following note.

6. For an analysis of Wood's rule reaching a conclusion contrary to Feinman's, that Wood was correct in his reading of prior cases, see

1

Freed & Polsby, The Doubtful Provenance of "Wood's Rule" Revisited, 22 Ariz.St.L.J. 551 (1990).

Part II

ESTABLISHING THE EMPLOYMENT RELATIONSHIP

Chapter 3

THE HIRING PROCESS

B. LEGAL RESTRICTIONS ON ACCESS TO JOBS

2. UNDOCUMENTED ALIENS

Page 107. Please add the following notes.

2A. Does an employer's failure to verify an alien's documentation before employment constitute constructive knowledge of the alien's unauthorized status in violation of IRCA? See Collins Food International, Inc. v. U.S. INS, 948 F.2d 549 (9th Cir.1991) (held: no).

8. Do employer sanctions under IRCA increase employment discrimination based on national origin? See Schwabach, Employer Sanctions and Discrimination: The Case for Repeal of the Employer Sanctions Provisions of the Immigration Reform and Control Act of 1986, 4 La Raza L.J. 1 (1991).

C. THE EMPLOYER'S INFORMATION–GATHERING PROCESS

2. INTERVIEWS

Page 122. Please add the following note.

7. A county veterans service agency was interviewing candidates for the position of director of the agency. When Maureen Barbano interviewed for the position, one of the members of the interviewing committee told her that he would not consider "some woman" for the position; he also asked what her plans were for having a family and whether her husband would object to her transporting male veterans. The Second Circuit held that the county violated Title VII by rejecting her application. Barbano v. Madison County, 922 F.2d 139 (2d Cir. 1990). Suppose that, despite the discriminatory interview, the applicant is found to be unqualified for the position. Has the employer violated Title VII? See Mitchell v. Jones Truck Lines, Inc., 754 F.Supp. 584 (W.D.Tenn.1990) (held: no).

4. NEGLIGENT HIRING

Page 137.   Please add the following to the end of note 1.

See Moore v. St. Joseph Nursing Home, Inc., 184 Mich.App. 766, 459 N.W.2d 100 (1990) (former employer had no duty to disclose former employee's dangerous proclivities to inquiring prospective employer).

Page 137.   Please add the following to the end of note 2.

Do public policy concerns for encouraging innovative release and rehabilitation programs for juvenile criminal offenders lessen an employer's duty to screen out dangerous employees? See Nigg v. Patterson, 233 Cal.App.3d 171, 276 Cal.Rptr. 587 (1990) (held: no), review granted 279 Cal.Rptr. 99, 806 P.2d 841 (1991).

Page 137.   Please add the following to the end of note 6.

Would B & L be liable if Harbour sexually assaulted a hotel clerk rather than a hitchhiker? See Connes v. Molalla Transport Systems, Inc., 817 P.2d 567 (Colo.App.1991) (held: no liability under theory of negligent entrustment).

D. TRUTH–DETECTING DEVICES AND PSYCHOLOGICAL AND PERSONALITY TESTS

2. OTHER TRUTH–DETECTING DEVICES AND PSYCHOLOGICAL AND PERSONALITY TESTS

Page 152.   Please add the following case after note 4.

SOROKA v. DAYTON HUDSON CORP.
235 Cal.App.3d 654, 1 Cal.Rptr.2d 77 (1991), review granted
4 Cal.Rptr.2d 180, 822 P.2d 1327 (1992).

REARDON, ASSOCIATE JUSTICE.

Appellants Sibi Soroka, Sue Urry and William d'Arcangelo filed a class action challenging respondent Dayton Hudson Corporation's practice of requiring Target Store security officer applicants to pass a psychological screening. The trial court denied Soroka's motion for a preliminary injunction to prohibit the use of this screening pending the outcome of this litigation. It also denied Soroka's motion for class certification and granted Dayton Hudson Corporation's motion to deny class certification. Soroka appeals from these orders, contending that a preliminary injunction should issue because he is likely to prevail on the merits of his constitutional and statutory claims. He also urges us to find that the trial court should have certified the class. The American Civil Liberties Union (ACLU) filed an amicus brief in support of Soroka's constitutional right to privacy claims. We reverse the trial court's order denying a preliminary injunction and remand the matter to the trial court for further proceedings on class certification.

FACTS

Respondent Dayton Hudson Corporation owns and operates Target Stores throughout California and the United States. Job applicants for store security officer (SSO) positions must, as a condition of employment, take a psychological test that Target calls the "Psychscreen." An SSO's main function is to observe, apprehend and arrest suspected shoplifters. An SSO is not armed, but carries handcuffs and may use force against a suspect in self-defense. Target views good judgment and emotional stability as important SSO job skills. It intends the Psychscreen to screen out SSO applicants who are emotionally unstable, who may put customers or employees in jeopardy, or who will not take direction and follow Target procedures.

The Psychscreen is a combination of the Minnesota Multiphasic Personality Inventory and the California Psychological Inventory. Both of these tests have been used to screen out emotionally unfit applicants for public safety positions such as police officers, correctional officers, pilots, air traffic controllers and nuclear power plant operators. The test is composed of 704 true-false questions. At Target, the test administrator is told to instruct applicants to answer every question.

The test includes questions about an applicant's religious attitudes, such as: "[¶] 67. I feel sure that there is only one true religion .... [¶] 201. I have no patience with people who believe there is only one true religion .... [¶] 477. My soul sometimes leaves my body .... [¶] 483. A minister can cure disease by praying and putting his hand on your head .... [¶] 486. Everything is turning out just like the prophets of the Bible said it would .... [¶] 505. I go to church almost every week. [¶] 506. I believe in the second coming of Christ .... [¶] 516. I believe in a life hereafter .... [¶] 578. I am very religious (more than most people) .... [¶] 580. I believe my sins are unpardonable .... [¶] 606. I believe there is a God .... [¶] 688. I believe there is a Devil and a Hell in afterlife."

The test includes questions that might reveal an applicant's sexual orientation, such as: "[¶] 137. I wish I were not bothered by thoughts about sex .... [¶] 290. I have never been in trouble because of my sex behavior .... [¶] 339. I have been in trouble one or more times because of my sex behavior .... [¶] 466. My sex life is satisfactory .... [¶] 492. I am very strongly attracted by members of my own sex .... [¶] 496. I have often wished I were a girl. (Or if you are a girl) I have never been sorry that I am a girl .... [¶] 525. I have never indulged in any unusual sex practices .... [¶] 558. I am worried about sex matters

.... [¶] 592. I like to talk about sex .... [¶] 640. Many of my dreams are about sex matters." [5]

An SSO's completed test is scored by the consulting psychologist firm of Martin–McAllister. The firm interprets test responses and rates the applicant on five traits: emotional stability, interpersonal style, addiction potential, dependability and reliability, and socialization—i.e., a tendency to follow established rules. Martin–McAllister sends a form to Target rating the applicant on these five traits and recommending whether to hire the applicant. Hiring decisions are made on the basis of these recommendations, although the recommendations may be overridden. Target does not receive any responses to specific questions. It has never conducted a formal validation study of the Psychscreen, but before it implemented the test, Target tested 17 or 18 of its more successful SSO's.

Appellants Sibi Soroka, Susan Urry and William d'Arcangelo were applicants for SSO positions when they took the Psychscreen. All three were upset by the nature of the Psychscreen questions. Soroka was hired by Target. Urry—a Mormon—and d'Arcangelo were not hired. In August 1989, Soroka filed a charge that use of the Psychscreen discriminated on the basis of race, sex, religion and physical handicap with the Department of Fair Employment and Housing.

Having exhausted their administrative remedies, Soroka, Urry and d'Arcangelo filed a class action against Target in September 1989 to challenge its use of the Psychscreen. The complaint was amended twice. The second amended complaint alleged that the test asked invasive questions that were not job-related. Soroka alleged causes of action for violation of the constitutional right to privacy, invasion of privacy, disclosure of confidential medical information, fraud, negligent misrepresentation, intentional and negligent infliction of emotional distress, violation of the Fair Employment and Housing Act, violation of sections 1101 and 1102 of the Labor Code, and unfair business practices. This complaint prayed for both damages and injunctive relief.

In June 1990, Soroka moved for a preliminary injunction to prohibit Target from using the Psychscreen during the pendency of the action. A professional psychologist submitted a declaration opining that use of the test was unjustified and improper, resulting in faulty assessments to the detriment of job applicants. He concluded that its use violated basic professional standards and that it had not been demonstrated to be reliable or valid as an employment evaluation. For example, one of the two tests on which the Psychscreen was based was designed for use only in hospital or clinical settings. Soroka noted that two of Target's

---

5. Soroka challenges many different types of questions on appeal. However, we do not find it necessary to consider questions other than those relating to religious beliefs and sexual orientation.

experts had previously opined that the Minnesota Multiphasic Personality Inventory was virtually useless as a preemployment screening device. It was also suggested that the Psychscreen resulted in a 61 percent rate of false positives—that is, that more than 6 in 10 qualified applicants for SSO positions were not hired.

Target's experts submitted declarations contesting these conclusions and favoring the use of the Psychscreen as an employment screening device. Some Target officials believed that use of this test has increased the quality and performance of its SSO's. However, others testified that they did not believe that there had been a problem with the reliability of SSO applicants before the Psychscreen was implemented. Target's vice president of loss prevention was unable to link changes in asset protection specifically to use of the Psychscreen. In rebuttal, Soroka's experts were critical of the conclusions of Target's experts. One rebuttal expert noted that some of the intrusive, non-job-related questions had been deleted from a revised form of the test because they were offensive, invasive and added little to the test's validity.

The trial court denied Soroka's motion to certify the class and granted Target's motion to deny class certification. The court concluded that the case was not an appropriate one for certification because of the predominantly individual nature of the claims. It found no well-defined community of interest among class members. The court also denied the motion because it could not conclude that the class would be fairly and adequately represented by Soroka, Urry, d'Arcangelo and their counsel, although it noted that counsel was extremely qualified in employment litigation. The court stated that because Soroka's answers to the Psychscreen test that he took had twice been made public, that disclosure would likely be an issue of substantial import to the invasion of privacy claims at trial.

The trial court also denied Soroka's motion for preliminary injunction. It ruled that he had not demonstrated a reasonable probability of prevailing on the merits of the constitutional or statutory claims at a trial. The court found that Target demonstrated a legitimate interest in psychologically screening applicants for security positions to minimize the potential danger to its customers and others. It also found that Target's practice of administering this test to SSO applicants was not unreasonable. Finally, the trial court denied both parties' motions for summary adjudication. This appeal followed.

* * *

A. *Constitutional Claim*

First, Soroka argues that he is likely to prevail at trial on his constitutional right to privacy claim. The parties dispute the standard to be applied to determine whether Target's violation of Soroka's privacy was justified. In order to understand the various legal issues underlying this contention, a review of the basic legal concepts that guide us is in order.

1. The Right to Privacy

The California Constitution explicitly protects our right to privacy. Article I, section 1 provides: "All people are by nature free and independent and have inalienable rights. Among these are enjoying and defending life and liberty, acquiring, possessing, and protecting property, and pursuing and obtaining safety, happiness, and privacy." "By this provision, California accords privacy the constitutional status of an inalienable right, on a par with defending life and possessing property." Before this constitutional amendment was enacted, California courts had found a state and federal constitutional right to privacy even though such a right was not enumerated in either constitution, and had consistently given a broad reading to the right to privacy. Thus, the elevation of the right to privacy to constitutional stature was intended to expand, not contract, privacy rights.

Target concedes that the Psychscreen constitutes an intrusion on the privacy rights of the applicants, although it characterizes this intrusion as a limited one. However, even the constitutional right to privacy does not prohibit *all* incursion into individual privacy. The parties agree that a violation of the right to privacy may be justified, but disagree about the standard to be used to make this determination. At trial, Target persuaded the court to apply a reasonableness standard because Soroka was an applicant, rather than a Target employee. On appeal, Soroka and the ACLU contend that Target must show more than reasonableness—that it must demonstrate a compelling interest— to justify its use of the Psychscreen.

2. Applicants vs. Employees

Soroka and the ACLU contend that job applicants are entitled to the protection of the compelling interest test, just as employees are. The trial court disagreed, employing a reasonableness standard enunciated in a decision of Division Three of this District which distinguished between applicants and employees.

In Wilkinson v. Times Mirror Corp., 215 Cal.App.3d 1034, 264 Cal.Rptr. 194 (1989), a book publisher required job applicants to submit to drug urinalysis as part of its preemployment physical examination. The appellate court rejected the applicants' contention that the compelling interest test should apply to determine whether the publisher's invasion of their privacy interests was justified under article I, section 1. Instead, the court fashioned and applied a lesser standard based on whether the challenged conduct was reasonable. When setting this standard, the most persuasive factor for the *Wilkinson* court appears to have been that the plaintiffs were applicants for employment rather than employees. "Any individual who chooses to seek employment necessarily also chooses to disclose certain personal information to prospective employers, such as employment and educational history, and to allow the prospective employer to verify that information." This applicant-employee distinction was pivotal for the *Wilkinson* court. "Simply put, applicants for jobs . . . have a choice; they may consent to the limited invasion of their privacy resulting from the testing, or may decline both the test and the conditional offer of employment."

Our review of the ballot argument satisfies us that the voters did not intend to grant less privacy protection to job applicants than to employees. The ballot argument specifically refers to job applicants when it states that Californians "are required to report some information, regardless of our wishes for privacy or our belief that there is no public need for the information. Each time we . . . *interview for a job,* . . . a dossier is opened and an informational profile is sketched." (Ballot Pamp., Proposed Amends. to Cal. Const. with arguments to voters, Gen. Elec. (Nov. 7, 1972) p. 27, emphasis added.) Thus, the major underpinning of *Wilkinson* is suspect.

Appellate court decisions predating *Wilkinson* have also applied the compelling interest standard in cases involving job applicants. Target attempts to distinguish these cases as ones involving public, not private, employers, but that is a distinction without a difference in the context of the state constitutional right to privacy. Private and public employers alike are bound by the terms of the privacy provisions of article I, section 1.

The legislative history and the prior California law are sufficient to convince us that no distinction should be made between the privacy rights of job applicants and employees.

* * *

Nevertheless, Target argues that this court has already embraced *Wilkinson*'s reasonableness standard and its distinction between applicants and employees. In Luck v. Southern Pacific Transportation Co., 218 Cal.App.3d 1, 267 Cal.Rptr. 618 (1990), this Division held that an employer's termination of a computer operator who refused to submit to drug urinalysis constituted a violation of the employee's right to privacy. In a footnote, we noted that *Wilkinson* applied the reasonableness test in a case involving a job applicant. We distinguished *Wilkinson,* stating that as the plaintiff in *Luck* was an "employee, rather than a job applicant, we are satisfied that the termination of her employment was a sufficient burden on her right to privacy to merit application of the compelling interest test." Target contends that this footnote constitutes an acceptance of *Wilkinson*'s reasonableness standard and an endorsement of a privacy distinction between job applicants and employees. We disagree. The cited language noted the holding in *Wilkinson* and found that case factually distinguishable; it did not embrace the *Wilkinson* analysis. As we found the compelling interest standard to apply to the employee before us in *Luck,* we were not required to consider—and did not determine—whether the same or a different standard would have applied had the plaintiff been a job applicant.

In conclusion, we are satisfied that any violation of the right to privacy of job applicants must be justified by a compelling interest. This conclusion is consistent with the voter's expression of intent when they amended article I, section 1 to make privacy an inalienable right and with subsequent decisions of the California Supreme Court.

3. *Nexus Requirement*

Soroka and the ACLU also argue that Target has not demonstrated that its Psychscreen questions are job-related—i.e., that they provide information relevant to the emotional stability of its SSO applicants. Having considered the religious belief and sexual orientation questions carefully, we find this contention equally persuasive.

Although the state right of privacy is broader than the federal right, California courts construing article I, section 1 have looked to federal precedents for guidance. Under the lower federal standard, employees may not be compelled to submit to a violation of their right to privacy unless a clear, direct nexus exists between the nature of the employee's duty and the nature of the violation. We are satisfied that this nexus requirement applies with even greater force under article I, section 1.

Again, we turn to the voter's interpretation of article I, section 1. The ballot argument—the only legislative history for the privacy amendment—specifically states that one purpose of the constitutional right to privacy is to prevent businesses "from collecting ... *unnecessary* information about us ...." It also asserts that the right to privacy would "preclude the collection of *extraneous* or *frivolous* information." (Ballot Pamp., Proposed Amends. to Cal. Const. with arguments to voters, Gen. Elec. (Nov. 7, 1972) p. 28, emphasis added.) Thus, the ballot language requires that the information collected be *necessary* to achieve the purpose for which the information has been gathered. This language convinces us that the voters intended that a nexus requirement apply.

The California Supreme Court has also recognized this nexus requirement. When it found that public employees could not be compelled to take a polygraph test, it criticized the questions asked as both highly personal and unrelated to any employment duties. It found that a public employer may require its workers to answer *some* questions, but only those that specifically, directly and narrowly relate to the performance of the employee's official duties. This nexus requirement also finds support in the seminal case from our high court on the right to privacy, which characterizes as one of the principal mischiefs at which article I, section 1 was directed "the *overbroad* collection ... of unnecessary personal information ...." If the information Target seeks is not job-related, that collection is overbroad, and the information unnecessary.

Wilkinson attempted to address this nexus requirement but its conclusion is inconsistent with federal law, which affords less protection than that provided by the state constitutional privacy amendment. *Wilkinson* held that an employer has a legitimate interest in not hiring individuals whose drug abuse may render them unable to perform their job responsibilities in a satisfactory manner. Federal courts have held that this sort of generalized justification is not sufficient to justify an infringement of an employee's Fourth Amendment rights. If this justification is insufficient to satisfy a lesser Fourth Amendment test, then it cannot pass muster under the more stringent compelling interest test.

4. *Application of Law*

Target concedes that the Psychscreen intrudes on the privacy interests of its job applicants. Having carefully considered *Wilkinson,* we find its reasoning unpersuasive. As it is inconsistent with both the legislative history of article I, section 1 and the case law interpreting that provision, we decline to follow it. Under the legislative history and case law, Target's intrusion into the privacy rights of its SSO applicants must be justified by a compelling interest to withstand constitutional scrutiny. Thus, the trial court abused its discretion by committing an error of law—applying the reasonableness test, rather than the compelling interest test.

While Target unquestionably has an interest in employing emotionally stable persons to be SSO's, testing applicants about their religious beliefs and sexual orientation does not further this interest. To justify the invasion of privacy resulting from use of the Psychscreen, Target must demonstrate a compelling interest and must establish that the test serves a job-related purpose. In its opposition to Soroka's motion for preliminary injunction, Target made no showing that a person's religious beliefs or sexual orientation have any bearing on the emotional stability or on the ability to perform an SSO's job responsibilities. It did no more than to make generalized claims about the Psychscreen's relationship to emotional fitness and to assert that it has seen an overall improvement in SSO quality and performance since it implemented the Psychscreen. This is not sufficient to constitute a compelling interest, nor does it satisfy the nexus requirement. Therefore, Target's inquiry into the religious beliefs and sexual orientation of SSO applicants unjustifiably violates the state constitutional right to privacy. Soroka has established that he is likely to prevail on the merits of his constitutional claims.

B. *Statutory Claims*

Soroka also contends that he is likely to prevail on the merits of his statutory claims. He makes two statutory claims—one based on the Fair Employment and Housing Act (FEHA) and another based on the Labor Code. As we have already found that portions of the Psychscreen as administered to Target's SSO applicants violate the constitutional right to privacy, it is not necessary for us to address the statutory issues to resolve the question of whether the preliminary injunction should issue. However, for the benefit of the trial court at the later trial, we will address these statutory claims.

1. *Fair Employment and Housing Act*

Soroka contends that the trial court abused its discretion by concluding that he was unlikely to prevail on his FEHA claims. These claims are based on allegations that the questions require applicants to divulge information about their religious beliefs. In its ruling on Soroka's motion for summary adjudication, the trial court found that he did not establish that Target's hiring decisions were based on religious beliefs, nor that the questions asked in the Psychscreen were designed to reveal such beliefs.

In California, an employer may not refuse to hire a person on the basis of his or her religious beliefs. Likewise, an employer is prohibited from making any non-job-related inquiry that expresses "directly or indirectly, any limitation, specification, or discrimination as to . . . religious creed . . . ." FEHA guidelines provide that an employer may make any preemployment inquiry that does not discriminate on a basis enumerated in FEHA. However, inquiries that identify an individual on the basis of religious creed are unlawful unless pursuant to a permissible defense. Job-relatedness is an affirmative defense. A means of selection that is facially neutral but that has an adverse impact on persons on the basis of religious creed is permissible only on a showing that the selection process is sufficiently related to an essential function of the job in question to warrant its use.

The trial court committed an error of law when it found that questions such as "I feel sure that there is only one true religion," "Everything is turning out just like the prophets of the Bible said it would," and "I believe in the second coming of Christ" were not intended to reveal religious beliefs. Clearly, these questions were intended to—and did—inquire about the religious beliefs of Target's SSO applicants. As a matter of law, these questions constitute an inquiry that expresses a "specification [of a] religious creed."

Once Soroka established a prima facie case of an impermissible inquiry, the burden of proof shifted to Target to demonstrate that the religious beliefs questions were job-related. As we have already determined, Target has not established that the Psychscreen's questions about religious beliefs have any bearing on that applicant's ability to perform an SSO's job responsibilities. Therefore, Soroka has established the likelihood that he will prevail at trial on this statutory claim.[10]

2. *Labor Code Sections 1101 and 1102*

Soroka also argues that the trial court abused its discretion by concluding that he was unlikely to prevail on his claims based on sections 1101 and 1102 of the Labor Code. The trial court found that Soroka did not establish that the questions asked in the Psychscreen are designed to reveal an applicant's sexual orientation. It also found that Soroka did not establish that Target's hiring decisions are made on the basis of sexual orientation.

Under California law, employers are precluded from making, adopting or enforcing any policy that tends to control or direct the political activities or affiliations of employees. Employers are also prohibited from coercing, influencing, or attempting to coerce or influence employees to adopt or follow or refrain from adopting or following any particular line of political activity by threatening a loss of employment. These statutes have been held to protect applicants as well as employees.

Labor Code sections 1101 and 1102 protect an employee's fundamental right to engage in political activity without employer interference. The "struggle of the homosexual community for equal rights, particularly in the field of employment, must be recognized as a political activity." These statutes also prohibit a private employer from discriminating against an employee on the basis of his or her sexual orientation.

The trial court committed an error of law when it determined that Psychscreen questions such as "I am very strongly attracted by members of my own sex" were not intended to reveal an applicant's sexual orientation. On its face, this question directly asks an applicant to reveal his or her sexual orientation. One of the five traits that Target uses the Psychscreen to determine is "socialization," which it defines as "the extent to which an individual subscribes to traditional values and mores and feels an obligation to act in accordance with them." Persons who identify themselves as homosexuals may be stigmatized as "willing to defy or violate" these norms, which may in turn result in an invalid test.

---

10. Soroka also challenges questions relating to physical handicaps or conditions. As we find that use of the Psychscreen violates FEHA regulations against questioning about an applicant's religious beliefs, we need not address these additional claims of error.

As a matter of law, this practice tends to discriminate against those who express a homosexual orientation. It also constitutes an attempt to coerce an applicant to refrain from expressing a homosexual orientation by threat of loss of employment. Therefore, Soroka has established that he is likely to prevail at trial on this statutory basis, as well.

* * *

CONCLUSION

Target's preemployment requirement of psychological screening violates both the constitutional right to privacy and statutory prohibitions against improper preemployment inquiries and discriminatory conduct by inquiring into its applicants' religious beliefs and sexual orientation. At trial, Soroka is likely to prevail on the merits of his complaint. The interim harm to Soroka and others if the preliminary injunction does not issue outweighs the harm to Target from being precluded from giving the Psychscreen in its present form during the pendency of this litigation.

The order denying the preliminary injunction is reversed. The order denying Soroka's motion for class certification and granting Target's motion to deny class certification is remanded to the trial court for further proceedings in accordance with this opinion. Target shall bear all costs on appeal, the amount of which shall be fixed by the trial court.

Notes and Questions

1. Assuming that the use of the Psychscreen does not have a disparate impact along the lines of religion or sexual orientation, should the entire test be banned because of certain of the numerous questions? Cf. Connecticut v. Teal, 457 U.S. 440 (1982) (5–4 decision rejecting "bottom line" defense). Should only those questions be banned?

2. Would it be lawful under Title VII for the employer to ask applicants what their religion and sexual orientation was on an application form if it did not use the information in making employment decisions?

3. Why should the employer have to demonstrate a compelling interest in the use of the test?

F. DRUG TESTING AND OTHER LABORATORY PROCEDURES

2. HIV TESTING

Page 203. Please add the following note.

3. Compare *Glover* with Anonymous Fireman v. City of Willoughby, 779 F.Supp. 402 (N.D. Ohio 1991) (upholding mandatory HIV testing

of fire fighters and paramedics as part of their annual physical exam, rejecting challenges under the fourth, ninth, and fourteenth amendments).

3. GENETIC TESTING

Page 208. Please add the following note.

5. The most recently enacted genetic discrimination laws are those of Oregon (1989), New York (1990), and Wisconsin (1992). Oregon prohibits employers from requiring applicants or employees to undergo "genetic screening," although the term is not further defined. Or.Rev. Stat. § 659.227. New York prohibits genetic discrimination based on sickle cell trait, Tay–Sachs trait, or Cooley's anemia trait. 1990 N.Y.Laws ch. 900. Wisconsin prohibits an employer from performing genetic testing or using the results of a genetic test. 1991 Wis.Act 117. For a further discussion, see Rothstein, Genetic Discrimination in Employment and the Americans with Disabilities Act, 29 Hous.L.Rev. ___ (1992).

Chapter 4

DISCRIMINATION IN HIRING

A. DISCRIMINATION ON THE BASIS OF RACE OR SEX

1. SOURCES OF PROTECTION

Page 220. Please insert the following at line 13.

Patterson was overturned by the Civil Rights Act of 1991.

2. WHAT IS UNLAWFUL DISCRIMINATION?

Page 247. Please add the following to the end of note 1.

The district court award was upheld on appeal. Hopkins v. Price Waterhouse, 920 F.2d 967 (D.C.Cir.1990).

Page 247. Please substitute the following for note 6.

6. The Civil Rights Act of 1991 responded to *Price Waterhouse* by allowing an unlawful employment practice to be established "when the complaining party demonstrates that race, color, religion, sex, or national origin was a motivating factor for any employment practice, even though other factors also motivated the practice." 42 U.S.C. § 2000e–2(m). Is this standard different from that proposed in earlier, unsuccessful legislation which would have established liability if the plaintiff could show that impermissible factors *contributed* to the employment practice?

Page 258. Please substitute for note 9.

9. The Civil Rights Act of 1991 overturned *Wards Cove*'s formulation of the burden of proof and the types of proof necessary to show disparate impact discrimination. Under the Act, an employee must still attempt to show which employment practice has caused the disparate impact. If, however, the practices are impossible to disaggregate, courts must analyze the decisionmaking process as one practice. In addition, Congress increased the burden on the employer in demonstrating that a challenged practice is job-related. Now, the employer must show that "the challenged practice is job-related for the position in question and consistent with business necessity." The burden of persuasion remains with the employer to prove business necessity.

16

Page 258. Please insert after the new note 9.

Note on the Civil Rights Act of 1991

A battle which began early in 1990 finally came to a close on November 21, 1991, when President Bush signed the Civil Rights Act of 1991. The purpose of the legislation—to overturn several Supreme Court decisions on civil rights and to grant victims of discrimination money damages under Title VII—had provoked bitter debates between the White House and the advocates of the bill. Over eighteen months, both sides introduced numerous bills, including one passed by Congress but successfully vetoed by the President. The new law addresses issues presented in Griggs v. Duke Power Co., p. 222; Price Waterhouse v. Hopkins, p. 238; Wards Cove Packing Co. v. Atonio, p. 249; Meritor Savings Bank, FSB v. Vinson, p. 502; and several cases noted in the book.

The enactment of the new civil rights law did not end the debates, however. For example, both Republicans and Democrats argue that their versions of legislative history should govern future court decisions.

The courts were immediately faced with another difficult issue— whether the Civil Rights Act of 1991 should apply to pending cases or only to cases filed after the Act became law. In light of numerous requests to amend complaints brought under Title VII, courts have had to decide whether plaintiffs who filed suit before the Act was passed can amend their claims to capture the benefits of the new bill. Sponsors of the legislation had expressed widely differing opinions on this issue, rendering the legislative history ambiguous.

Seeking guidance, district courts have looked to Supreme Court precedent. But with two conflicting lines of authority over the presumptive retroactivity or prospectivity of a statute, the Supreme Court's decisions provide no clear direction to the lower courts. Thus, the district courts have looked to whether the circuit in which they sit follows Bowen v. Georgetown University Hospital, 488 U.S. 204 (1988) (holding that congressional enactments are presumptively prospective) or Bradley v. School Board of City of Richmond, 416 U.S. 696 (1974) (intervening statute applies unless a contrary intention appears or the application would result in manifest injustice).

In Mojica v. Gannett Co., 779 F.Supp. 94 (N.D.Ill.1991), the Northern District of Illinois ruled in favor of retroactivity. Allowing the plaintiff to amend her claim to add compensatory damages, punitive damages, and a jury trial, the court held that *Bradley* was the favored precedent in the Seventh Circuit. Thus, according to the court, unless such a reading would create a manifest injustice or there was congressional intent to the contrary, the court would presume that the Act was to be applied retroactively. Finding the language and the legislative history inconclusive, the court turned to the question of manifest injustice. The court looked to three factors. "1) the nature and identity of the parties; 2) the nature of the rights affected; and 3) the impact of the change in law on pre-existing rights." Noting the public concern with the issue of discrimination, the court found that the putative private nature of the suit would not require prospectivity. Second, the court found that the defendant had no right to a bench trial, but that the plaintiff's right to a jury trial was "entitled to substantial protection." Moreover, the court found that the defendant's behavior had been illegal before the Act was passed, and thus the rights and obligations of the parties were not affected. The mere increase in damages would not have altered the conduct of the parties.

Several other district courts have followed the reasoning of the *Mojica* opinion. See, e.g., Stender v. Lucky Stores, Inc., 780 F.Supp. 1302 (N.D.Cal.1992). One court, finding the right to a jury trial to be purely procedural, allowed the plaintiff to amend her complaint. See King v. Shelby Medical Center, 779 F.Supp. 157 (N.D.Ala.1991). See also Great American Tool & Manufacturing Co. v. Adolph Coors Co., 780 F.Supp. 1354 (D.Colo.1992) (allowing application of Act to conduct occurring before enactment where case was filed after passage of the Act).

Reaching the opposite conclusion, the District Court for the District of Columbia held that the Act does not apply retroactively. Van Meter v. Barr, 778 F.Supp. 83 (D.D.C.1991). The court declared that the right to seek compensatory damages was substantive in nature. Thus, following *Bowen*, the court held the Act presumptively prospective. Finding no statutory language or legislative history to counter the presumption, the court denied the plaintiff's request to amend his complaint. See also Hansel v. Public Service Co., 778 F.Supp. 1126 (D.Colo.1991); Alexandre v. AMP, Inc., 1991 WL 322947 (W.D.Pa.1991).

Page 259. Please add the following note.

10.   On remand, the district court held that the plaintiffs failed to prove that the company's hiring practices had a disparate impact on their job opportunities. Atonio v. Wards Cove Packing Co., ___ F.Supp. ___, 54 FEP Cases 1623 (W.D.Wash.1991).

3. THE BONA FIDE OCCUPATIONAL QUALIFICATION DEFENSE

Page 267. Please add the following to note 4.

Is sex a BFOQ for the jobs of manager, assistant manager, and instructor at Women's Workout World, an all-female health club? See EEOC v. Sedita, 755 F.Supp. 808 (N.D.Ill.1991) (held: no). Accord, Jennings v.

New York State Office of Mental Health, 786 F.Supp. 376 (S.D.N.Y. 1992) (gender BFOQ in assignments of personal attendants in state residential mental health facility).

4. ENFORCEMENT AND REMEDIES

Page 283. Please add the following at the end of note 4.

The Civil Rights Act of 1991 responded to this decision by making consent decrees much more difficult to challenge.

B. DISCRIMINATION BASED ON FACTORS OTHER THAN RACE OR SEX

1. RELIGION

Page 299. Please add the following after note 7.

7A. Is it unlawful religious discrimination for an employer to require that management employees attend a week-long seminar on "interpersonal relationships" which draws heavily on the scriptures? See Kolodziej v. Smith, 412 Mass. 215, 588 N.E.2d 634 (1992) (held: no).

2. NATIONAL ORIGIN

Page 306. Please add the following to note 6.

See Janko v. Illinois State Toll Highway Authority, 704 F.Supp. 1531 (N.D.Ill.1989) ("Gypsy" is a national origin for Title VII purposes).

Page 306. Please add the following to note 7.

Wards Cove was altered, and arguably overturned, by the Civil Rights Act of 1991.

See generally Perea, English–Only Rules and the Right to Speak One's Primary Language in the Workplace, 23 U.Mich.J.L.Ref. 265 (1990).

Page 307. Please add the following to note 10.

In EEOC v. Arabian American Oil Co., 111 S.Ct. 1227 (1991), the Supreme Court held that Title VII does not apply extraterritorially to regulate employment practices of U.S. employers that employ U.S. citizens abroad. This decision was overturned by the Civil Rights Act of 1991. Both Title VII and the Americans with Disabilities Act now apply to American citizens working for American businesses abroad.

Page 308. Please add the following note.

12. In EEOC v. Tortilleria "La Mejor," 758 F.Supp. 585 (E.D.Cal. 1991), the court held that Title VII covers undocumented aliens and that their coverage was not affected by the enactment of IRCA.

3. AGE

Page 315. Please add the following to note 2.

See Kaminshine, The Cost of Older Workers, Disparate Impact, and the Age Discrimination in Employment Act, 42 Fla.L.Rev. 229 (1990).

Page 315. Please add the following to note 5.

Can an employer be liable for age discrimination based on its refusal to hire an applicant because he was "overqualified"? See Taggart v. Time Inc., 924 F.2d 43 (2d Cir.1991) (held: yes). But see Stein v. National City Bank, 942 F.2d 1062 (6th Cir.1991) (no violation of ADEA for bank to refuse to consider college graduates for customer service representative position).

Page 316. Please add the following note.

8. In Gilmer v. Interstate/Johnson Lane Corp., 111 S.Ct. 1647 (1991), the Supreme Court held that an employee's ADEA claim was barred because he had signed an agreement specifying that arbitration was the remedy for any controversy arising out of his employment or the termination of his employment. The Sixth Circuit has since applied the Supreme Court's reasoning to a Title VII claim. See Willis v. Dean Witter Reynolds, Inc., 948 F.2d 305 (6th Cir.1991).

Page 316. Please add the following note.

9. Should back pay awards be counted as taxable income? See Downey v. Commissioner, 97 T.C. 150 (1991) (reversing its prior decision which had considered award received in settlement of a claim under the ADEA to be taxable income).

4. DISABILITY

Page 324. Please add the following to note 6.

State disabilities laws sometimes have broader definitions of disability and therefore may be more protective of gender identity conditions. See Doe v. Boeing Co., 64 Wash.App. 235, 823 P.2d 1159 (1992) (held: gender dysphoria (transsexualism) is a "handicap").

Page 325. Please add the following at the end of note 7.

Some courts have held extreme sensitivity to smoke to be a handicap. In County of Fresno v. Fair Employment & Housing Commission, 226 Cal.App.3d 1541, 277 Cal.Rptr. 557 (1991), the court upheld the California Fair Employment and Housing Commission's (FEHC) determination that Fresno County had failed to reasonably accommodate two employees' hypersensitivity to tobacco smoke. But see Pletten v. Merit Systems Protection Board, 908 F.2d 973 (6th Cir.1990) (upholding the MSPB's determination that Pletten did not meet the criteria of "qualified handicapped individual" because to accommodate the plaintiff's need for a totally smoke-free environment was not reasonable). See also Hall v. Turnage, 946 F.2d 895 (6th Cir.1991) (same).

Page 325. Please add the following to the end of note 8.

Does reasonable accommodation include allowing a computer programmer with multiple sclerosis to work at home? See Langon v. Department of Health & Human Services, 959 F.2d 1053 (D.C.Cir.1992) (§ 501 of Rehabilitation Act may require permitting home work).

5. SEXUAL ORIENTATION

Page 342. Please add the following to note 4.

Connecticut, New Jersey, and Vermont now also prohibit discrimination in employment based on sexual orientation.

Page 342. Please add the following note.

5. In Jantz v. Muci, 759 F.Supp. 1543 (D.Kan.1991), a public school teacher was denied employment because of the principal's perception that he had "homosexual tendencies." The teacher, who was married with two children, apparently reminded the principal's secretary of her husband, whom she believed was a homosexual. The court held that discrimination on the basis of sexual orientation, as opposed to conduct, is subject to heightened constitutional scrutiny, under which the school's action could not be justified. Even if the rational basis test were used, the school board still failed to offer any rational basis for its action.

Page 342. Please add the following note.

6. The Georgia Attorney General withdrew the job offer of a lesbian attorney when it became known that she planned to marry another woman and take her name. Is the withdrawal of the job offer unconstitutional? See Shahar v. Bowers, ___ F.Supp. ___ (N.D.Ga.1992) (denying defendant's motion to dismiss).

Part III

TERMS AND CONDITIONS OF EMPLOYMENT

Chapter 5

WAGES, HOURS, AND BENEFITS

A. STATE AND FEDERAL WAGE AND HOUR REGULATION

1. FEDERAL WAGE AND HOUR REGULATION: THE FAIR LABOR STANDARDS ACT

Page 356. Please omit the main case and substitute the following case.

DALHEIM v. KDFW–TV
918 F.2d 1220 (5th Cir.1990).

ALVIN B. RUBIN, CIRCUIT JUDGE:

* * *

Plaintiffs are nineteen present and former general-assignment reporters, producers, directors, and assignment editors employed in the news and programming departments of television station KDFW–TV (KDFW). As its call letters imply, KDFW serves the Dallas–Fort Worth area which, with approximately 3.5 million viewers, is the eighth largest television market in the nation. The news and programming departments are responsible for producing KDFW's local news broadcasts and its public affairs programming.

KDFW's general-assignment reporters usually receive a new coverage assignment each day. The assignment manager or an assignment editor tells the reporter the story to be covered, what she is expected to "shoot," and the intended angle or focus of the story. After the reporter interviews the persons that she or another KDFW employee has arranged to interview, she obtains pertinent video footage, and then writes and records the text of the story, subject to review by the producer. Some reporters help assemble the video and text narration; others rely on a video editor to put the final package together. General-assignment reporters are only infrequently assigned to do a series of reports focusing on a single topic or related topics. Successful reporters usually have a pleasant physical appearance and a strong and appeal-

22

ing voice, and are able to present themselves as credible and knowledgeable.

Producers are responsible for determining the content of the ten-to-twelve minute news portion of KDFW's thirty-minute newscast. They participate in meetings to decide which stories and story angles will be covered; they also decide the amount of time to be given a particular story, the sequence in which stories will be aired, and when to take commercial breaks. Producers have the authority to revise reporters' stories. All of the producers' actions are subject to approval by the executive producer.

Directors review the script for the newscast in order to prepare technical instructions for "calling" the show. The director decides which camera to use and on which machine to run videotaped segments or preproduction graphics. During the broadcast, the director cues the various technical personnel, telling them precisely when to perform their assigned tasks. The overall appearance of KDFW's newscasts, however, is prescribed by station management. The director therefore has no discretion concerning lighting, camera-shot blocking, closing-shot style, or the sequence of opening and closing graphics. KDFW's directors also direct some public affairs programming, which have no prescribed format but involve only simple camera work and a basic set. In addition, KDFW's directors screen commercials to be aired by the station to ensure that they meet the standards set by KDFW's parent, Times Mirror Corporation.

Assignment editors are primarily responsible for pairing reporters with both photographers and videotape editors. They also monitor the wire services, police and fire department scanners, newspapers, and press releases for story ideas that conform to KDFW's general guidelines. Assignment editors have no authority to decide the stories to be covered, but they may reassign reporters if they learn of a story requiring immediate action. Assignment editors operate under the supervision of the assignment manager.

Plaintiffs brought this suit in May, 1985, alleging that KDFW's reporters, producers, directors, and assignment editors were required to work more than forty hours per week without overtime pay, in willful violation of § 7 of the FLSA, and seeking to recover back wages from May, 1982 to the present. After an eight-day bench trial, the district court concluded that none of the plaintiffs was exempt from § 7 as a bona fide executive, administrative, or professional employee under § 13(a)(1) and that KDFW had violated the FLSA by failing to pay overtime. The court further concluded, however, that KDFW's violation was not willful, and that KDFW therefore was not liable for damages outside the FLSA's two-year statute of limitations for nonwillful violations.

Section 7 of the FLSA requires employers to pay overtime to employees who work more than forty hours per week. Section 13(a)(1) exempts from the maximum hour provision employees occupying "bona fide executive, administrative, or professional" positions. That same section empowers the Secretary of Labor to define by regulation the terms "executive," "administrative," and "professional." She has done so at 29 C.F.R. § 541.0 et seq., setting out "long" tests for employees earning more than $155 per week but less than $250 per week, which include specific criteria, and "short" tests, described in less detail, for employees earning more than $250 per week. In addition, the Secretary has issued interpretations of those regulations, which are codified at 29 C.F.R. § 541.100 et seq. The § 13(a)(1) exemptions are "construed narrowly against the employer seeking to assert them," and the employer bears the burden of proving that employees are exempt.

The short test for the executive exemption requires that an employee's "primary duty" consist of the "management of the enterprise" in which she is employed "or a customarily recognized subdivision thereof." In addition, the executive employee's work must include "the customary and regular direction of the work" of two or more employees. The regulations define an exempt administrative employee as one whose "primary duty" consists of "office or nonmanual work directly related to management policies or general business operations" that "includes work requiring the exercise of discretion and independent judgment." The exemption for creative professionals requires that the employee's "primary duty" consist of work that is "original and creative in character in a recognized field of artistic endeavor," the result of which depends "primarily on the invention, imagination, or talent of the employee."

KDFW challenges the holding of the district court on four distinct grounds, claiming that the district court (1) erroneously construed the term "primary duty" to mean duties occupying more than half of an employee's time; (2) erroneously concluded that reporters' work is not "original and creative" as those terms are used in the regulations; (3) misconstrued the requirement that administrative work be "directly related to management policies and general business operations," in that it (a) erroneously applied the concept of "production," as that term is used in the Secretary's interpretations, to the work of white-collar employees like producers, directors, and assignment editors, and (b) erroneously concluded that the work of producers, directors, and assignment editors should not be deemed "directly related" to business operations because they "carr[y] out major assignments in conducting the operations of the business," within the meaning of the interpretations; and (4) erroneously failed to "tack" exemptions for producers, directors, and assignment editors as provided for in the regulations.

* * *

IV

A. *KDFW's General–Assignment Reporters*

KDFW argues that its general-assignment reporters are exempt artistic professionals. Under the regulations, KDFW must prove that the reporter's "primary duty" consists of work that is "original and creative in character in a recognized field of artistic endeavor," the result of which depends "primarily on the invention, imagination, or talent of the employee."

The regulations and interpretations at issue here, §§ 541.3(a)(2) and 541.303(e) and (f), have not changed in any material respect since 1949, long before broadcast journalism evolved into its modern form. To apply the Secretary's interpretation literally to the plaintiffs would be to assume that those occupations exist today as they did forty years ago. No one disputes that the technological revolution that has swept this society into the so-called Information Age has rendered that assumption untenable. The question is what role, if any, § 541.303(e) and (f) may have in determining the exempt status of modern broadcast journalists.

KDFW argues that the district court gave the interpretation undue weight, thus blinding itself to the realities of modern broadcast journalism. Rather than focusing on the "essential nature" of reporters' duties, KDFW contends, the district court "pigeonholed" reporters according to standards that are decades out of date. Amicus National Association of Broadcasters (NAB) goes even further, contending that the Secretary's interpretation is based on "erroneous, outmoded assumptions about journalism and journalists," and that "[i]nsofar as the District Court took these 1940 assumptions about print journalists and applied them to the present-day duties of KDFW television reporters, [it] erred as a matter of law."

* * *

The Secretary's interpretations make it abundantly clear that § 541.3(a)(2) was intended to distinguish between those persons whose work is creative in nature from those who work in a medium capable of bearing creative expression, but whose duties are nevertheless functional in nature. The factual inquiry in this case was directed precisely at determining on which side of that line KDFW's reporters stand. The district court found that, at KDFW, the emphasis was on "good reporting, in the aggregate," and not on individual reporters with the "presence" to draw an audience. The district court found that the process by which reporters meld sound and pictures relies not upon the reporter's creativity, but upon her skill, diligence, and intelligence. More importantly, the district court found that "[r]eporters are told the story that the station intends they cover, what they are expected to shoot, and the intended angle or focus of the story."

In essence, the district court found that KDFW failed to prove that the work constituting its reporters' primary duty is original or creative in character. The district court recognized, and we think correctly, that general-assignment reporters may be exempt creative professionals, and that KDFW's reporters did, from time to time, do original and creative work. Nevertheless, at KDFW, the approach reporters take to their day-to-day work is in large part dictated by management, and the stories they daily produce are neither analytic nor interpretive nor original. In neither form nor substance does a reporter's work "depend[ ] primarily on [her] invention, imagination, or talent." Those inferences, while not compelled by the evidence, are certainly supported by it. Based on those inferences and the underlying historical facts, which we review only for clear error, we think the legal conclusion that reporters are nonexempt follows as a matter of course. We therefore conclude that the district court did not err in holding that KDFW's general-assignment reporters are not exempt professionals.

B. *KDFW's News Producers*

KDFW argues that its news producers are exempt either as creative professionals, administrators, executives, or a combination thereof. We address each argument in turn.

1. *Producers as Creative Professionals.*—KDFW does not press this argument much, for good reason. The district court found that KDFW failed to prove that the work producers do in rewriting reporters' copy and in formatting the newscast are products of their "invention, imagination, and talent." Rather, producers perform their work within a well-defined framework of management policies and editorial convention. To the extent that they exercise discretion, it is governed more by skill and experience than by originality and creativity. Because the district court's findings are supported by the record, we find no error.

2. *Producers as Administrators.*—The argument KDFW pursues most vigorously with respect to producers is that they are exempt administrative employees. Section 541.2 of the regulations requires that an exempt administrator perform (1) office or nonmanual work (2) that is directly related to the employer's management policies or general business operations and (3) involves the exercise of discretion and independent judgment. The Secretary's interpretation, § 541.-205(a), defines the "directly related" prong by distinguishing between what it calls "the administrative operations of a business" and "production." Administrative operations include such duties as "advising the management, planning, negotiating, representing the company, purchasing, promoting sales, and business research and control." Work may also be "directly related" if it is of "substantial importance" to the business operations of the enterprise in that it involves "major assignments in conducting the operations of the business, or ... affects business operations to a substantial degree." KDFW argues that the

district court erred in finding that producers' work failed the "directly related" requirement because it is neither related to the administrative operations of KDFW, nor is it of "substantial importance" to the enterprise. Whether an employee's work is or should be deemed "directly related" to business operations is an inference drawn from the historical facts; we review such inferences for clear error.

* * *

That is not the case with KDFW's news producers. Their responsibilities begin and end with the ten-to-twelve minute portion of the newscast they are working on. They are not responsible for setting business policy, planning the long- or short-term objectives of the news department, promoting the newscast, negotiating salary or benefits with other department personnel, or any of the other types of "administrative" tasks noted in § 541.205(b). The district court determined, based on the facts before it, that "[t]he duties of a producer clearly relate to the production of a KDFW news department product and not to defendant's administrative operations." That determination was not erroneous.

KDFW next asserts that the district court erred in holding that producers' work does not consist of carrying out "major assignments" of "substantial importance" to KDFW's business. Again, KDFW disputes the district court's factual conclusions and inferences, and again, its contention is without merit. KDFW was charged with proving that its producers are exempt employees. The only record evidence KDFW points to in support of its contention that producers' work is of "substantial importance," other than the evidence of what producers do, is that KDFW operates in the nation's eighth largest television market, and that local news is an important source of revenue for the station. The "importance" of producers' work we are left to infer is that, if a producer performs poorly, KDFW's bottom line might suffer.

As a matter of law, that is insufficient to establish the direct relationship required by § 541.2 by virtue of the "substantial importance" contemplated by § 541.205(c). The Secretary's interpretations specifically recognize that the fact that a worker's poor performance may have a significant profit-and-loss impact is not enough to make that worker an exempt administrator. "An employee's job can even be 'indispensable' and still not be of the necessary 'substantial importance' to meet the 'directly related' element." In assessing whether an employee's work is of substantial importance, it is necessary yet again to look to "the *nature* of the work, not its ultimate consequence." The nature of producers' work, the district court found, is the application of "techniques, procedures, repetitious experience, and specific standards" to the formatting of a newscast. KDFW was obliged to demonstrate how work of that nature is so important to KDFW that it should be deemed "directly related" to business operations. It did not do so.

Indeed, the evidence shows that the work one would think of as being "substantially important"—such as setting news department policy and designing the uniform "look" of the newscast—is done by employees who seem clearly to be exempt administrators: the executive producer and the news director, for example. We therefore conclude that the district court did not err in holding that producers are not exempt administrators.

3. *Producers as Executives.*—

* * *

To qualify for an executive exemption under the short test, an employee's primary duty must consist of the "management of the enterprise" in which she is employed "or a customarily recognized subdivision thereof." In addition, the employee must customarily and regularly direct the work of two or more employees. The district court found that management was not the producers' primary duty, and that producers do not customarily direct the work of two or more employees.

We agree with the district court. The evidence establishes that, while the producer plays an important role in coordinating and formatting a portion of the newscast, the other members of the ensemble—that is, the reporters, technicians, assignment editors, and so on—are actually supervised by other management personnel. Producers perform none of the executive duties contemplated by the regulations, such as training, supervising, disciplining, and evaluating employees. Indeed, this court previously upheld a determination by the National Labor Relations Board that neither producers nor directors nor assignment editors are "supervisors" within § 2(11) of the National Labor Relations Act. Producers, therefore, do not "manage," and are not exempt executives.

* * *

C. *KDFW's Directors and Assignment Editors*

For the same reasons it asserts with respect to its producers, KDFW claims that the district court erred in concluding that its directors and assignment editors are not exempt either as executives or administrators or a combination thereof. KDFW's arguments with respect to directors and assignment editors thus fail for the reasons set out above. First, the evidence wholly fails to establish that the work of either directors or assignment editors is "directly related" to management policies or business operations, as required by § 541.2. Second, the evidence does not demonstrate that either directors or assignment editors "manage" anything, as required by § 541.1. KDFW's directors are, as the district court found, highly skilled coordinators, but they are not managers. Assignment editors have no real authority, and participate in no decisions of consequence. Finally, because neither directors nor assignment editors do any exempt work, the district court did not err in failing to consider a combination exemption under § 541.600.

For the reasons stated above, the judgment of the district court is AFFIRMED.

Page 366. Please add the following to note 4.

In Blanton v. City of Murfreesboro, 856 F.2d 731 (6th Cir.1988), the court found that the city's downward adjustment of firefighters' base wage rate to offset the increased cost imposed by the Act violated the FLSA regardless of the city's good faith.

Page 371. Please add the following to the end of note 6.

In Bouchard v. Regional Governing Board, 939 F.2d 1323 (8th Cir.1991), cert. denied 112 S.Ct. 1761 (1992), the court held employees of a Nebraska institution for the mentally retarded, who were required to sleep on the premises, were not entitled to overtime compensation for sleep time.

A somewhat different result was reached in Johnson v. Columbia, 949 F.2d 127 (4th Cir.1991), where the court held that an "express agreement" to exclude sleep and meal time from compensable work hours is not enforceable under the FLSA when the "agreement" was extracted under threat of termination. Such exclusions must be consensual.

Page 379. Please add the following to the end of note 7.

The Labor Department recently issued new regulations on hazardous occupations for minors. The changes (1) eliminate the exemption for minors under 18 to work as school bus drivers; (2) explicitly prohibit restaurants, fast-food establishments, and other retail establishments from allowing minors to use power-driven meat processing equipment; (3) provide that power-driven meat slicers are meat processing equipment under the regulations; and (4) expressly prohibit minors under 18 from using power-driven paper machinery in the processing of paper.

B. WHAT IS A JOB WORTH?

2. WAGE COMPARABILITY FOR INDIVIDUALS: THE QUEST FOR PAY EQUITY

Page 418. Please add the following as note e.

e. A federal employer hires a man with disabilities and four women and proceeds to pay the male employee significantly more. The male employee's eligibility for a special exception to normal Civil Service hiring criteria was found to be a factor other than sex. Girdis

v. EEOC, 688 F.Supp. 40 (D.Mass.1987), affirmed 851 F.2d 540 (1st Cir.1988).

Page 419. Please add the following to note 8.

The Tax Court recently overruled its prior decisions which had found such benefits taxable. Downey v. Commissioner, 97 T.C. 150 (1991).

Page 437. Please add the following to note 9.

Washington State's program has had some setbacks. For example, traditional women's jobs have remained segregated but with better pay. Although no employees have suffered pay reductions to finance the plan, the state has decreased cost-of-living adjustments. And the state has been forced to grant special pay increases to keep employees with special skills from leaving state employ to join the higher-paying private sector. Peter T. Kilborn, Wage Gap Between Sexes is Cut in Test, but at a Price, New York Times, May 31, 1990, at A1, col. 1.

C. FRINGE BENEFITS

2. STATUTORY PROVISION AND PROTECTION OF BENEFITS

Page 452. Please add the following note.

7. The Third Circuit has recently upheld an employer's right unilaterally to reduce severance pay benefits below the level specified in its benefits handbook. In Hamilton v. Air Jamaica, Ltd., 945 F.2d 74 (3d Cir.1991), cert. denied 112 S.Ct. 1479 (1992), the court held that ERISA does not bar an employer from making case-by-case employee benefit decisions when the plan expressly reserves this right to the employer.

Page 458. Please add the following note.

5. In Conkwright v. Westinghouse Electric Corp., 933 F.2d 231 (4th Cir.1991), the Fourth Circuit held that § 510 of ERISA provides a cause of action to fully vested employees who claim to have been prevented from accruing additional benefits.

Page 458. Please add the following case before *Metropolitan Life*.

McGANN v. H & H MUSIC CO.
946 F.2d 401 (5th Cir.1991), petition for cert. filed, 60 U.S.L.W. 3582 (1992).

GARWOOD, CIRCUIT JUDGE:

Plaintiff-appellant John McGann (McGann) filed this suit under section 510 of the Employee Retirement Income Security Act of 1974 (ERISA), against defendants-appellees H & H Music Company (H & H Music), Brook Mays Music Company (Brook Mays) and General American Life Insurance Company (General American) (collectively defendants) claiming that they discriminated against McGann, an employee of H & H Music, by reducing benefits available to H & H Music's group medical plan beneficiaries for treatment for acquired immune deficiency syndrome (AIDS) and related illnesses. The district court granted defendants' motion for summary judgment on the ground that an employer has an absolute right to alter the terms of medical coverage available to plan beneficiaries. We affirm.

FACTS AND PROCEEDINGS BELOW

McGann, an employee of H & H Music, discovered that he was afflicted with AIDS in December 1987. Soon thereafter, McGann submitted his first claims for reimbursement under H & H Music's group medical plan, provided through Brook Mays, the plan administrator, and issued by General American, the plan insurer, and informed his employer that he had AIDS. McGann met with officials of H & H Music in March 1988, at which time they discussed McGann's illness. Before the change in the terms of the plan, it provided for lifetime medical benefits of up to $1,000,000 to all employees.

In July 1988, H & H Music informed its employees that, effective August 1, 1988, changes would be made in their medical coverage. These changes included, but were not limited to, limitation of benefits payable for AIDS-related claims to a lifetime maximum of $5,000.[1] No limitation was placed on any other catastrophic illness. H & H Music became self-insured under the new plan and General American became the plan's administrator. By January 1990, McGann had exhausted the $5,000 limit on coverage for his illness.

In August 1989, McGann sued H & H Music, Brook Mays and General American under section 510 of ERISA, which provides, in part, as follows:

"It shall be unlawful for any person to discharge, fine, suspend, expel, discipline, or discriminate against a participant or beneficiary for exercising any right to which he is entitled under the provisions of an employee benefit plan, ... or for the purpose of interfering with the attainment of any right to which such participant may become entitled under the plan ..."

McGann claimed that defendants discriminated against him in violation of both prohibitions of section 510.[2] He claimed that the provision limiting coverage for AIDS-related expenses was directed specifically at him in retaliation for exercising his rights under the

---

1. Other changes included increased individual and family deductibles, elimination of coverage for chemical dependency treatment, adoption of a preferred provider plan and increased contribution requirements.

2. McGann also asserted various state law claims which the district court dismissed without discussion. McGann's brief in this court states that he "does not appeal from that part of the [district] court's order."

medical plan and for the purpose of interfering with his attainment of a right to which he may become entitled under the plan.

Defendants, conceding the factual allegations of McGann's complaint, moved for summary judgment.[3] These factual allegations include no assertion that the reduction of AIDS benefits was intended to deny benefits to McGann for any reason which would not be applicable to other beneficiaries who might then or thereafter have AIDS, but rather that the reduction was prompted by the knowledge of McGann's illness, and that McGann was the only beneficiary then known to have AIDS.[4] On June 26, 1990, the district court granted defendants' motion on the ground that they had an absolute right to alter the terms of the plan, regardless of their intent in making the alterations. The district court also held that even if the issue of discriminatory motive were relevant, summary judgment would still be proper because the defendants' motive was to ensure the future existence of the plan and not specifically to retaliate against McGann or to interfere with his exercise of future rights under the plan.

DISCUSSION

McGann contends that defendants violated both clauses of section 510 by discriminating against him for two purposes: (1) "for exercising any right to which [the beneficiary] is entitled," and (2) "for the purpose of interfering with the attainment of any right to which such participant may become entitled." In order to preclude summary judgment in defendants' favor, McGann must make a showing sufficient to establish the existence of a genuine issue of material fact with respect to each material element on which he would carry the burden of proof at trial.

At trial, McGann would bear the burden of proving the existence of defendants' specific discriminatory intent as an essential element of either of his claims. Thus, in order to survive summary judgment McGann must make a showing sufficient to establish that a genuine issue exists as to defendants' specific intent to retaliate against McGann for filing claims for AIDS-related treatment or to interfere with McGann's attainment of any right to which he may have become entitled.

Although we assume there was a connection between the benefits reduction and either McGann's filing of claims or his revelations about

---

3. General American claimed that the district court should have dismissed it as a defendant with respect to McGann's ERISA claim because ERISA does not create a cause of action against a nonemployer and McGann has never been employed by General American. Because of our disposition of this appeal on alternative grounds, we do not find it necessary to address this issue.

4. We assume, for purposes of this appeal that the defendants' knowledge of McGann's illness was a motivating factor in their decision to reduce coverage for AIDS-related expenses, that this knowledge was obtained either through McGann's filing of claims or his meetings with defendants, and that McGann was the only plan beneficiary then known to have AIDS.

his illness, there is nothing in the record to suggest that defendants' motivation was other than as they asserted, namely to avoid the expense of paying for AIDS treatment (if not, indeed, also for other treatment), no more for McGann than for any other present or future plan beneficiary who might suffer from AIDS. McGann concedes that the reduction in AIDS benefits will apply equally to all employees filing AIDS-related claims and that the effect of the reduction will not necessarily be felt only by him. He fails to allege that the coverage reduction was otherwise specifically intended to deny him particularly medical coverage except "in effect." He does not challenge defendants' assertion that their purpose in reducing AIDS benefits was to reduce costs.

Furthermore, McGann has failed to adduce evidence of the existence of "any right to which [he] may become entitled under the plan." The right referred to in the second clause of section 510 is not simply any right to which an employee may conceivably become entitled, but rather any right to which an employee may become entitled pursuant to an existing, enforceable obligation assumed by the employer. "Congress viewed [section 510] as a crucial part of ERISA because, without it, employers would be able to circumvent the provision of *promised* benefits."

McGann's allegations show no *promised* benefit, for there is nothing to indicate that defendants ever promised that the $1,000,000 coverage limit was permanent. The H & H Music plan expressly provides: "Termination or Amendment of Plan: The Plan Sponsor may terminate or amend the Plan at any time or terminate any benefit under the Plan at any time." There is no allegation or evidence that any oral or written representations were made to McGann that the $1,000,000 coverage limit would never be lowered. Defendants broke no promise to McGann. The continued availability of the $1,000,000 limit was not a right to which McGann may have become entitled for the purposes of section 510.[5] To adopt McGann's contrary construction of this portion of section 510 would mean that an employer could not effectively reserve the right to amend a medical plan to reduce benefits respecting subsequently incurred medical expenses, as H & H Music did here, because such an amendment would obviously have as a purpose preventing participants from attaining the right to such future benefits as they otherwise might do under the existing plan absent the amendment. But this is plainly not the law, and ERISA does not require such "vesting" of the right to a continued level of the same medical benefits once those are ever included in a welfare plan.

---

5. McGann does not claim that he was not fully reimbursed for all claimed medical expenses incurred on or prior to August 1, 1988; or that the full $5,000 has not been made available to him in respect to AIDS related medical expenses incurred by him on or after July 1, 1988.

McGann appears to contend that the reduction in AIDS benefits alone supports an inference of specific intent to retaliate against him or to interfere with his future exercise of rights under the plan. McGann characterizes as evidence of an individualized intent to discriminate the fact that AIDS was the only catastrophic illness to which the $5,000 limit was applied and the fact that McGann was the only employee known to have AIDS. He contends that if defendants reduced AIDS coverage because they learned of McGann's illness through his exercising of his rights under the plan by filing claims, the coverage reduction therefore could be "retaliation" for McGann's filing of the claims.[6] Under McGann's theory, any reduction in employee benefits would be impermissibly discriminatory if motivated by a desire to avoid the anticipated costs of continuing to provide coverage for a particular beneficiary. McGann would find an implied promise not to discriminate for this purpose; it is the breaking of this promise that McGann appears to contend constitutes interference with a future entitlement.

McGann cites only one case in which a court has ruled that a change in the terms and conditions of an employee-benefits plan could constitute illegal discrimination under section 510. Vogel v. Independence Federal Sav. Bank, 728 F.Supp. 1210 (D.Md.1990). In *Vogel*, however, the plan change at issue resulted in the plaintiff and only the plaintiff being excluded from coverage. McGann asserts that the *Vogel* court rejected the defendant's contention that mere termination of benefits could not constitute unlawful discrimination under section 510, but in fact the court rejected this claim not because it found that mere termination of coverage could constitute discrimination under section 510, but rather because the termination at issue affected only the beneficiary. Nothing in *Vogel* suggests that the change there had the potential to then or thereafter exclude any present or possible future plan beneficiary other than the plaintiff. *Vogel* therefore provides no support for the proposition that the alteration or termination of a medical plan could alone sustain a section 510 claim. Without necessarily approving of the holding in *Vogel*, we note that it is inapplicable to the instant case. The post-August 1, 1988 $5,000 AIDS coverage limit applies to any and all employees.

McGann effectively contends that section 510 was intended to prohibit any discrimination in the alteration of an employee benefits plan that results in an identifiable employee or group of employees being treated differently from other employees. The First Circuit rejected a somewhat similar contention in Aronson v. Servus Rubber, Div. of Chromalloy, 730 F.2d 12 (1st Cir.), cert. denied, 469 U.S. 1017 (1984). In *Aronson*, an employer eliminated a profit sharing plan with

6. We assume that discovery of McGann's condition—and realization of the attendant, long-term costs of caring for McGann—did in fact prompt defendants to reconsider the $1,000,000 limit with respect to AIDS-related expenses and to reduce the limit for future such expenses to $5,000.

respect to employees at only one of two plants. The disenfranchised employees sued their employer under section 510, claiming that partial termination of the plan with respect to employees at one plant and not at the other constituted illegal discrimination. The court rejected the employees' discrimination claim, stating in part:

> "[Section 510] relates to discriminatory conduct directed against individuals, not to actions involving the plan in general. The problem is with the word 'discriminate.' An overly literal interpretation of this section would make illegal any partial termination, since such terminations obviously interfere with the attainment of benefits by the terminated group, and, indeed, are expressly intended so to interfere .... This is not to say that a plan could not be discriminatorily modified, intentionally benefitting, or injuring, certain identified employees or a certain group of employees, but a partial termination cannot constitute discrimination per se. A termination that cuts along independently established lines—here separate divisions—and that has a readily apparent business justification, demonstrates no invidious intent." Id. at 16 (citation omitted).

The Supreme Court has observed in dictum: "ERISA does not mandate that employers provide any particular benefits, and does not itself proscribe discrimination in the provision of employee benefits." To interpret "discrimination" broadly to include defendants' conduct would clearly conflict with Congress's intent that employers remain free to create, modify and terminate the terms and conditions of employee benefits plans without governmental interference.

* * *

As persuasively explained by the Second Circuit, the policy of allowing employers freedom to amend or eliminate employee benefits is particularly compelling with respect to medical plans:

> "With regard to an employer's right to change medical plans, Congress evidenced its recognition of the need for flexibility in rejecting the automatic vesting of welfare plans. Automatic vesting was rejected because the costs of such plans are subject to fluctuating and unpredictable variables. Actuarial decisions concerning fixed annuities are based on fairly stable data, and vesting is appropriate. In contrast, medical insurance must take account of inflation, changes in medical practice and technology, and increases in the costs of treatment independent of inflation. These unstable variables prevent accurate predictions of future needs and costs." Moore v. Metropolitan Life Ins. Co., 856 F.2d 488, 492 (2d Cir.1988).

In *Metropolitan Life,* the court rejected an ERISA claim by retirees that their employer could not change the level of their medical benefits without their consent. The court stated that limiting an employer's right to change medical plans increased the risk of "decreas[ing] protection for future employees and retirees."

McGann's claim cannot be reconciled with the well-settled principle that Congress did not intend that ERISA circumscribe employers' control over the content of benefits plans they offered to their employees. McGann interprets section 510 to prevent an employer from reducing or eliminating coverage for a particular illness in response to the escalating costs of covering an employee suffering from that illness. Such an interpretation would, in effect, change the terms of H & H Music's plan. Instead of making the $1,000,000 limit available for medical expenses on an as-incurred basis only as long as the limit remained in effect, the policy would make the limit *permanently* available for all medical expenses as they might thereafter be incurred because of a single event, such as the contracting of AIDS. Under McGann's theory, defendants would be effectively proscribed from reducing coverage for AIDS once McGann had contracted that illness and filed claims for AIDS-related expenses. If a federal court could prevent an employer from reducing an employee's coverage limits for AIDS treatment once that employee contracted AIDS, the boundaries of judicial involvement in the creation, alteration or termination of ERISA plans would be sorely tested.

As noted, McGann has failed to adduce any evidence of defendants' specific intent to engage in conduct proscribed by section 510. A party against whom summary judgment is ordered cannot raise a fact issue simply by stating a cause of action where defendants' state of mind is a material element.

Proof of defendants' specific intent to discriminate among plan beneficiaries on grounds not proscribed by section 510 does not enable McGann to avoid summary judgment. ERISA does not broadly prevent an employer from "discriminating" in the creation, alteration or termination of employee benefits plans; thus, evidence of such intentional discrimination cannot alone sustain a claim under section 510. That section does not prohibit welfare plan discrimination between or among categories of diseases. Section 510 does not mandate that if some, or most, or virtually all catastrophic illnesses are covered, AIDS (or any other particular catastrophic illness) must be among them. It does not prohibit an employer from electing not to cover or continue to cover AIDS, while covering or continuing to cover other catastrophic illnesses, even though the employer's decision in this respect may stem from some "prejudice" against AIDS or its victims generally. The same, of course, is true of any other disease and its victims. That sort of "discrimination" is simply not addressed by section 510. Under section

510, the asserted discrimination is illegal only if it is motivated by a desire to retaliate against an employee or to deprive an employee of an existing right to which he may become entitled. The district court's decision to grant summary judgment to defendants therefore was proper. Its judgment is accordingly

AFFIRMED.

Notes and Questions

1. ERISA distinguishes between welfare benefit plans and pension plans, providing more stringent protections for the latter. The statute expressly excludes welfare plans from the stringent minimum vesting, participation, and funding standards imposed on pension plans. ERISA §§ 201(1), 301(a)(1), 29 U.S.C. §§ 1051(1), 1081(a)(1).

Courts, previous to the *McGann* case, had found that ERISA thus exempts welfare plans from any affirmative requirement of vesting. See Moore v. Metropolitan Life, 856 F.2d 488 (2d Cir.1988) (holding that ERISA does not require vesting of the right to a continued level of medical benefits included in welfare plan).

2. In Hamilton v. Air Jamaica, Ltd., 945 F.2d 74 (3d Cir.1991), cert. denied 112 S.Ct. 1479 (1992), the court applied a similar logic to find that the airline's reservation of rights to alter its severance pay policy was valid. Although the employee handbook specified four weeks of severance pay, it also contained a provision reserving Air Jamaica's right to amend its pay practices and any employment policies or benefits. One day before Hamilton's termination, the airline informed its employees of the change in severance policy in a memorandum which stated that the pay would amount to two weeks salary rather than four. The Third Circuit concluded that Air Jamaica had no obligation to provide a definite amount of severance pay and that the amendment of the plan (through its memorandum) was valid.

3. Does this differentiation between welfare plans and pension plans seem fair? One commentator has recommended that Congress amend ERISA to provide more protection for medical plans.

> Retiree insurance should be presumed a lifetime benefit which vests at retirement unless the employer includes in plan documents and employee handbooks an explicit and unambiguous termination clause indicating otherwise. Even if such a clause is included, it should not be enforced unless it permits reductions or termination only in the event that the company is in severe financial distress. Finally, to ensure that retirees receive their benefits, ... retiree insurance plans [should] be funded in ways similar to those in which pension plans are funded.

Joan Vogel, Until Death Do Us Part: Vesting of Retiree Insurance, 9 Indus.Rel.L.J. 183, 240 (1987).

Does this seem like a good solution?

4. Sometimes courts have been faced with welfare plans which have no explicit provision reserving the right to the employer to reduce or eliminate benefits. In the case of collectively bargained benefits, the court will look to the intent of the parties to determine if the benefits are to continue beyond the agreement's termination. When the language is ambiguous and the company's actions and statements indicate it did not consider the benefits to be limited to the duration of the collective bargaining agreement, the court will treat the benefits as guaranteed for the retiree's lifetime. See International Union (UAW) v. Yard–Man, Inc., 716 F.2d 1476 (6th Cir.1983), cert. denied 465 U.S. 1007 (1984). In construing ambiguous terms, the court may look to extrinsic evidence or to other sections in the contract.

Courts construing nonunion welfare benefit plans have similarly looked at the parties' intent. In re White Farm Equipment Co., 788 F.2d 1186 (6th Cir.1986) (parties may themselves set out by agreement or by private design, as set out in plan documents, whether retiree welfare benefits vest, or whether they may be terminated).

5. In *Yard–Man*, the court held that "when parties contract for benefits which accrue upon achievement of retiree status, there is an inference that the parties likely intended those benefits to continue as long as the beneficiary remains a retiree."

Does this inference find a basis in ERISA?

6. What promises do employers make to employees when they offer health "insurance" or health "benefits"? If employers were unable to amend their health benefits plans, what would be some of the likely consequences?

7. The effect of ERISA is to preempt some state laws regulating commercial health insurance. If state laws could be applied, what should those laws provide? That health insurance premiums may not be increased? That policies may not be cancelled? That all claims for illnesses incurred while a policy was in force must be paid for the duration of the illness?

Page 464. Please add the following to the end of note 1.

In Schwartz v. Newsweek, Inc., 653 F.Supp. 384 (S.D.N.Y.1986), affirmed 827 F.2d 879 (2d Cir.1987), the employer persuaded the court that its severance pay policy was governed by ERISA.

Page 465. Please add the following to the end of note 3.

The *McClendon* decision was reversed by the Supreme Court. Ingersoll–Rand Co. v. McClendon, 111 S.Ct. 478 (1990).

A District of Columbia statute, requiring employers who provide health insurance to employees to provide equivalent coverage to employees receiving workers' compensation benefits, was held to be preempted by ERISA. See Greater Washington Board of Trade v. District of Columbia, 948 F.2d 1317 (D.C.Cir.1991), cert. granted 112 S.Ct. 1584 (1992). But see R.R. Donnelly & Sons Co. v. Prevost, 915 F.2d 787 (2d Cir.1990), cert. denied 111 S.Ct. 1415 (1991) (ERISA does not preempt law requiring extension of health insurance coverage to employees receiving workers' compensation).

Page 465. Please add the following to the end of note 4.

Are an employee's claims for emotional distress, defamation, and invasion of privacy preempted by ERISA when the claim arose after co-workers accused her of committing a fraud on her employer by working part-time at another job while receiving disability payments from her original employer? See Thomas v. Telemecanique, Inc., 768 F.Supp. 503 (D.Md.1991) (held: yes).

Page 465. Please insert after new reference to *McClendon* in note 4.

See also Summers v. United States Tobacco Co., 214 Ill.App.3d 878, 158 Ill.Dec. 412, 574 N.E.2d 206 (1991) (claim alleging deceased husband was terminated to avoid paying health benefits preempted under ERISA).

Page 478. Please add the following to note 1.

State statutes which offer less protection than the PDA may be preempted, however. See O'Loughlin v. Pinchback, 579 So.2d 788 (Fla.App.1991).

Page 478. Please add the following to note 6.

May an employer prohibit a teacher from taking sick leave immediately before taking maternity leave under a policy that prohibits teachers from combining sick leave with any other form of leave? See Maganuco v. Leyden Community High School District 212, 939 F.2d 440 (7th Cir.1991) (held: yes).

Page 479. Please add the following to the end of note 8.

A male employee does have standing to sue an employer who discharges him because of the employee's wife's pregnancy. See Nicol v. Imagematrix, Inc., 773 F.Supp. 802 (E.D.Va.1991).

Page 479. Please add the following to the end of note 9.

More recently, the Seventh Circuit held that statistical evidence focusing on the absolute number of sick days used by female teachers during their teaching careers was insufficient, standing alone, to show that the school district's leave policies had a disparate impact on female teachers who experienced pregnancy-related disability. According to the court, "a statistical basis for this argument might have been established by showing that women who have been disabled due to pregnancy have accumulated sick days at a greater rate per year of service than their male coworkers or than women who have not experienced pregnancy-related disability." The court also found that a collectively bargained bar against taking maternity leave immediately following a disability leave did not discriminate by forcing women to choose between using accumulated sick days for pregnancy-related disability and taking maternity leave subsequent to birth. The policy did not depend on the biological fact of pregnancy and possible disability but on the teacher's choice to stay at home with her newborn child. Maganuco v. Leyden Community High School District 212, 939 F.2d 440 (7th Cir.1991).

Page 479. Please add the following notes.

11. An employer's policy denied medical and dental coverage to an employee's spouse if the spouse was the "head of the household." Does this policy violate Title VII under either a disparate treatment or disparate impact theory? See Colby v. J.C. Penney Co., 926 F.2d 645 (7th Cir.1991) (held: no).

12. In 1991 President Bush vetoed legislation (H.R. 2 and S. 2) that would have required large employers to grant workers 12 weeks of unpaid leave for birth, adoption, or family medical emergencies with continued health benefits.

There are currently 26 states with such laws, 14 applicable to the public and private sector and 12 applicable only in the public sector. The states vary in whether they require leave for the birth of a child, adoption, family illness (including the employee's own illness), or some combination of the three. The duration of the leave ranges from six weeks to two years. Most state laws provide that employees on leave can continue group health and other benefits at their own expense, while some states also specify which benefits must be extended and at what cost to the employee.

For an example of judicial construction of a state family leave law, see Butzlaff v. Wisconsin Personnel Commission, 166 Wis.2d 1028, 480 N.W.2d 559 (App.1992) (employee need not work for same employer for 52 consecutive weeks prior to leave); Kelley Co. v. Marquardt, 166 Wis.2d 45, 479 N.W.2d 185 (App.1991) (failure to return employee to equivalent position violates the law).

3. THE CHANGING NATURE OF BENEFITS: CONTAINING EMPLOYER COSTS, IMPROVING EMPLOYEE CHOICES

Page 482. Please add the following note.

3. Should employers be required to provide benefits for domestic partners if their benefits programs cover the spouses and dependents of employees?

Chapter 6

CONDITIONS OF EMPLOYMENT

A. WORK ENVIRONMENT

1. GROOMING AND DRESS

Page 494. Please add the following to note 4.

See also Gayle v. Human Rights Commission, 218 Ill.App.3d 109, 161 Ill.Dec. 17, 578 N.E.2d 144 (1991) (refusal to hire Jamaican born black man who was member of Rastafarian religion and whose hair was in dreadlocks was not discrimination based on race, religion, or national origin because there was inadequate evidence that the employer knew the reason why he wore dreadlocks).

Page 494. Please add the following to note 5.

Cf. Bradley v. Pizzaco of Nebraska, Inc., 926 F.2d 714 (8th Cir.1991) (no violation of Title VII where plaintiff had mild case of pseudofolliculitis barbae and was able to shave).

Page 495. Please add the following notes.

8. An employer had a rule prohibiting male employees from wearing facial jewelry, including earrings; female employees were permitted to wear facial jewelry that was not "unusual or overly large." Does this rule constitute sex discrimination in violation of a state fair employment law? See Lockhart v. Louisiana–Pacific Corp., 102 Or. App. 593, 795 P.2d 602 (1990) (held: no).

9. In 1991 American Airlines settled a lawsuit brought by its flight attendants, which alleged that the airline's weight standards discriminated on the basis of age and sex. Under the airline's former standards, any woman 5–foot–5 could weigh no more than 129 pounds. Under the new standards, a 25–year–old who is 5–foot–5 can weigh up to 136 pounds; a 55–year–old who is 5–foot–5 can weigh up to 154 pounds. For a general discussion of this issue, see Note, Flight Attendant Weight Policies: A Title VII Wrong Without a Remedy, 64 S.Cal. L.Rev. 175 (1990).

2. HARASSMENT

Page 512. Please add the following to note 9.

Rojo was affirmed by the Supreme Court of California. Rojo v. Kliger, 52 Cal.3d 65, 276 Cal.Rptr. 130, 801 P.2d 373 (1990).

See also Thoreson v. Penthouse International, Ltd., 149 Misc.2d 150, 563 N.Y.S.2d 968 (1990) (award of $60,000 compensatory damages and $4 million punitive damages in sexual harassment case).

Page 513.   Please add the following to the end of note 12.

Does the verbal and physical abuse of an employee by his coworkers because of their belief that he is homosexual constitute hostile environment sex discrimination under Title VII?   See Dillon v. Frank, 952 F.2d 403 (6th Cir.1992) (held: no).

Page 513.   Please add the following to note 13.

Patterson was overturned by the Civil Rights Act of 1991.

Page 513.   Please add the following notes.

14.   Whether sexual overtures or sexual horseplay were "unwelcome" often involves close questions of fact.   See, e.g., Kouri v. Liberian Services, Inc., ___ F.Supp. ___, 55 FEP Cases 124 (E.D.Va.1991) (no Title VII violation where plaintiff sent "mixed signals" by, among other things, exchanging gifts and notes with her supervisor); Weinsheimer v. Rockwell International Corp., 754 F.Supp. 1559 (M.D.Fla.1990) (no Title VII violation where plaintiff was a frequent and willing participant in sexual innuendo).

15.   In Carreno v. Electrical Workers, ___ F.Supp. ___, 54 FEP Cases 81 (D.Kan.1990), the court held that co-workers' alleged verbal and physical abuse relating to the employee's homosexual lifestyle was not "based on the employee's sex" and therefore did not constitute hostile environment sexual harassment under Title VII.

Page 513.   Please include the following case and notes after the above notes.

ELLISON v. BRADY
924 F.2d 872 (9th Cir.1991).

Beezer, Circuit Judge:

Kerry Ellison appeals the district court's order granting summary judgment to the Secretary of the Treasury on her sexual harassment action brought under Title VII of the Civil Rights Act of 1964.   This appeal presents two important issues: (1) what test should be applied to determine whether conduct is sufficiently severe or pervasive to alter the conditions of employment and create a hostile working environment, and (2) what remedial actions can shield employers from liability for sexual harassment by co-workers.   The district court held that Ellison did not state a prima facie case of hostile environment sexual harassment.   We reverse and remand....

I

Kerry Ellison worked as a revenue agent for the Internal Revenue Service in San Mateo, California. During her initial training in 1984 she met Sterling Gray, another trainee, who was also assigned to the San Mateo office. The two co-workers never became friends, and they did not work closely together.

Gray's desk was twenty feet from Ellison's desk, two rows behind and one row over. Revenue agents in the San Mateo office often went to lunch in groups. In June of 1986 when no one else was in the office, Gray asked Ellison to lunch. She accepted. Gray had to pick up his son's forgotten lunch, so they stopped by Gray's house. He gave Ellison a tour of his house.

Ellison alleges that after the June lunch Gray started to pester her with unnecessary questions and hang around her desk. On October 9, 1986, Gray asked Ellison out for a drink after work. She declined, but she suggested that they have lunch the following week. She did not want to have lunch alone with him, and she tried to stay away from the office during lunch time. One day during the following week, Gray uncharacteristically dressed in a three-piece suit and asked Ellison out for lunch. Again, she did not accept.

On October 22, 1986 Gray handed Ellison a note he wrote on a telephone message slip which read:

> I cried over you last night and I'm totally drained today. I have never been in such constant term oil (sic). Thank you for talking with me. I could not stand to feel your hatred for another day.

When Ellison realized that Gray wrote the note, she became shocked and frightened and left the room. Gray followed her into the hallway and demanded that she talk to him, but she left the building.

Ellison later showed the note to Bonnie Miller, who supervised both Ellison and Gray. Miller said "this is sexual harassment." Ellison asked Miller not to do anything about it. She wanted to try to handle it herself. Ellison asked a male co-worker to talk to Gray, to tell him that she was not interested in him and to leave her alone. The next day, Thursday, Gray called in sick.

Ellison did not work on Friday, and on the following Monday, she started four weeks of training in St. Louis, Missouri. Gray mailed her a card and a typed, single-spaced, three-page letter. She describes this letter as "twenty times, a hundred times weirder" than the prior note. Gray wrote, in part:

> I know that you are worth knowing with or without sex .... Leaving aside the hassles and disasters of recent weeks. I have enjoyed you so much over these past few months. Watching you. Experiencing you from O so far away. Admiring your style and

elan .... Don't you think it odd that two people who have never
even talked together, alone, are striking off such intense sparks ...
I will [write] another letter in the near future.[1]

Explaining her reaction, Ellison stated: "I just thought he was crazy. I
thought he was nuts. I didn't know what he would do next. I was
frightened."

She immediately telephoned Miller. Ellison told her supervisor
that she was frightened and really upset. She requested that Miller
transfer either her or Gray because she would not be comfortable
working in the same office with him. Miller asked Ellison to send a
copy of the card and letter to San Mateo.

Miller then telephoned her supervisor, Joe Benton, and discussed
the problem. That same day she had a counseling session with Gray.
She informed him that he was entitled to union representation. During this meeting, she told Gray to leave Ellison alone.

At Benton's request, Miller apprised the labor relations department of the situation. She also reminded Gray many times over the
next few weeks that he must not contact Ellison in any way. Gray
subsequently transferred to the San Francisco office on November 24,
1986. Ellison returned from St. Louis in late November and did not
discuss the matter further with Miller.

After three weeks in San Francisco, Gray filed union grievances
requesting a return to the San Mateo office. The IRS and the union
settled the grievances in Gray's favor, agreeing to allow him to transfer
back to the San Mateo office provided that he spend four more months
in San Francisco and promise not to bother Ellison. On January 28,
1987, Ellison first learned of Gray's request in a letter from Miller
explaining that Gray would return to the San Mateo office. The letter
indicated that management decided to resolve Ellison's problem with a
six-month separation, and that it would take additional action if the
problem recurred.

After receiving the letter, Ellison was "frantic." She filed a formal
complaint alleging sexual harassment on January 30, 1987 with the
IRS. She also obtained permission to transfer to San Francisco temporarily when Gray returned.

Gray sought joint counseling. He wrote Ellison another letter
which still sought to maintain the idea that he and Ellison had some
type of relationship.

The IRS employee investigating the allegation agreed with Ellison's
supervisor that Gray's conduct constituted sexual harassment. In its
final decision, however, the Treasury Department rejected Ellison's

---

1. In the middle of the long letter Gray did say "I am obligated to you so much that if you want me to leave you alone I will .... If you want me to forget you entirely, I can not do that."

complaint because it believed that the complaint did not describe a pattern or practice of sexual harassment covered by the EEOC regulations. After an appeal, the EEOC affirmed the Treasury Department's decision on a different ground. It concluded that the agency took adequate action to prevent the repetition of Gray's conduct.

Ellison filed a complaint in September of 1987 in federal district court. The court granted the government's motion for summary judgment on the ground that Ellison had failed to state a prima facie case of sexual harassment due to a hostile working environment. Ellison appeals.

II

Congress added the word "sex" to Title VII of the Civil Rights Act of 1964 at the last minute on the floor of the House of Representatives. Virtually no legislative history provides guidance to courts interpreting the prohibition of sex discrimination. In Meritor Savings Bank v. Vinson, the Supreme Court held that sexual harassment constitutes sex discrimination in violation of Title VII.

Courts have recognized different forms of sexual harassment. In "quid pro quo" cases, employers condition employment benefits on sexual favors. In "hostile environment" cases, employees work in offensive or abusive environments. This case, like *Meritor,* involves a hostile environment claim.

* * *

III

The parties ask us to determine if Gray's conduct, as alleged by Ellison, was sufficiently severe or pervasive to alter the conditions of Ellison's employment and create an abusive working environment. The district court, with little Ninth Circuit case law to look to for guidance, held that Ellison did not state a prima facie case of sexual harassment due to a hostile working environment. It believed that Gray's conduct was "isolated and genuinely trivial." We disagree.

* * *

Although *Meritor* and our previous cases establish the framework for the resolution of hostile environment cases, they do not dictate the outcome of this case. Gray's conduct falls somewhere between forcible rape and the mere utterance of an epithet. * * *

The government asks us to apply the reasoning of other courts which have declined to find Title VII violations on more egregious facts. In Scott v. Sears, Roebuck & Co., 798 F.2d 210, 212 (7th Cir.1986), the Seventh Circuit analyzed a female employee's working conditions for sexual harassment. It noted that she was repeatedly propositioned and winked at by her supervisor. When she asked for assistance, he asked "what will I get for it?" Co-workers slapped her buttocks and commented that she must moan and groan during sex. The court examined the evidence to see if "the demeaning conduct and sexual stereotyping cause[d] such anxiety and debilitation to the plaintiff that working conditions were 'poisoned' within the meaning of Title VII." The court did not consider the environment sufficiently hostile.

Similarly, in Rabidue v. Osceola Refining Co., 805 F.2d 611 (6th Cir.1986), cert. denied, 481 U.S. 1041, 107 S.Ct. 1983, 95 L.Ed.2d 823 (1987), the Sixth Circuit refused to find a hostile environment where the workplace contained posters of naked and partially dressed women, and where a male employee customarily called women "whores," "cunt," "pussy," and "tits," referred to plaintiff as "fat ass," and specifically stated, "All that bitch needs is a good lay." Over a strong dissent, the majority held that the sexist remarks and the pin-up posters had only a de minimis effect and did not seriously affect the plaintiff's psychological well-being.

We do not agree with the standards set forth in *Scott* and *Rabidue,* and we choose not to follow those decisions. Neither *Scott's* search for "anxiety and debilitation" sufficient to "poison" a working environment nor *Rabidue's* requirement that a plaintiff's psychological well-being be "seriously affected" follows directly from language in *Meritor.* It is the harasser's conduct which must be pervasive or severe, not the alteration in the conditions of employment. Surely, employees need not endure sexual harassment until their psychological well-being is seriously affected to the extent that they suffer anxiety and debilitation. Although an isolated epithet by itself fails to support a cause of action for a hostile environment, Title VII's protection of employees from sex discrimination comes into play long before the point where victims of sexual harassment require psychiatric assistance.

We have closely examined *Meritor* and our previous cases, and we believe that Gray's conduct was sufficiently severe and pervasive to alter the conditions of Ellison's employment and create an abusive working environment. We first note that the required showing of severity or seriousness of the harassing conduct varies inversely with the pervasiveness or frequency of the conduct.

Next, we believe that in evaluating the severity and pervasiveness of sexual harassment, we should focus on the perspective of the victim. If we only examined whether a reasonable person would engage in allegedly harassing conduct, we would run the risk of reinforcing the prevailing level of discrimination. Harassers could continue to harass merely because a particular discriminatory practice was common, and victims of harassment would have no remedy.

We therefore prefer to analyze harassment from the victim's perspective. A complete understanding of the victim's view requires, among other things, an analysis of the different perspectives of men and women. Conduct that many men consider unobjectionable may offend many women.

We realize that there is a broad range of viewpoints among women as a group, but we believe that many women share common concerns which men do not necessarily share.[9] For example, because women are disproportionately victims of rape and sexual assault, women have a stronger incentive to be concerned with sexual behavior. Women who are victims of mild forms of sexual harassment may understandably worry whether a harasser's conduct is merely a prelude to violent sexual assault. Men, who are rarely victims of sexual assault, may view sexual conduct in a vacuum without a full appreciation of the social setting or the underlying threat of violence that a woman may perceive.

In order to shield employers from having to accommodate the idiosyncratic concerns of the rare hyper-sensitive employee, we hold that a female plaintiff states a prima facie case of hostile environment sexual harassment when she alleges conduct which a reasonable woman [11] would consider sufficiently severe or pervasive to alter the conditions of employment and create an abusive working environment.[12]

We adopt the perspective of a reasonable woman primarily because we believe that a sex-blind reasonable person standard tends to be male-biased and tends to systematically ignore the experiences of women. The reasonable woman standard does not establish a higher level of protection for women than men. Instead, a gender-conscious examination of sexual harassment enables women to participate in the workplace on an equal footing with men. By acknowledging and not trivializing the effects of sexual harassment on reasonable women, courts can work towards ensuring that neither men nor women will

---

9. One writer explains: "While many women hold positive attitudes about uncoerced sex, their greater physical and social vulnerability to sexual coercion can make women wary of sexual encounters. Moreover, American women have been raised in a society where rape and sex-related violence have reached unprecedented levels, and a vast pornography industry creates continuous images of sexual coercion, objectification and violence. Finally, women as a group tend to hold more restrictive views of both the situation and type of relationship in which sexual conduct is appropriate. Because of the inequality and coercion with which it is so frequently associated in the minds of women, the appearance of sexuality in an unexpected context or a setting of ostensible equality can be an anguishing experience."

Abrams, Gender Discrimination and the Transformation of Workplace Norms, 42 Vand.L.Rev. 1183, 1205 (1989).

11. Of course, where male employees allege that co-workers engage in conduct which creates a hostile environment, the appropriate victim's perspective would be that of a reasonable man.

12. We realize that the reasonable woman standard will not address conduct which some women find offensive. Conduct considered harmless by many today may be considered discriminatory in the future. Fortunately, the reasonableness inquiry which we adopt today is not static. As the views of reasonable women change, so too does the Title VII standard of acceptable behavior.

have to "run a gauntlet of sexual abuse in return for the privilege of being allowed to work and make a living."

We note that the reasonable victim standard we adopt today classifies conduct as unlawful sexual harassment even when harassers do not realize that their conduct creates a hostile working environment. Well-intentioned compliments by co-workers or supervisors can form the basis of a sexual harassment cause of action if a reasonable victim of the same sex as the plaintiff would consider the comments sufficiently severe or pervasive to alter a condition of employment and create an abusive working environment.[13] That is because Title VII is not a fault-based tort scheme. "Title VII is aimed at the consequences or effects of an employment practice and not at the ... motivation" of co-workers or employers. To avoid liability under Title VII, employers may have to educate and sensitize their workforce to eliminate conduct which a reasonable victim would consider unlawful sexual harassment.

The facts of this case illustrate the importance of considering the victim's perspective. Analyzing the facts from the alleged harasser's viewpoint, Gray could be portrayed as a modern-day Cyrano de Bergerac wishing no more than to woo Ellison with his words. There is no evidence that Gray harbored ill will toward Ellison. He even offered in his "love letter" to leave her alone if she wished. Examined in this light, it is not difficult to see why the district court characterized Gray's conduct as isolated and trivial.

Ellison, however, did not consider the acts to be trivial. Gray's first note shocked and frightened her. After receiving the three-page letter, she became really upset and frightened again. She immediately requested that she or Gray be transferred. Her supervisor's prompt response suggests that she too did not consider the conduct trivial. When Ellison learned that Gray arranged to return to San Mateo, she immediately asked to transfer, and she immediately filed an official complaint.

We cannot say as a matter of law that Ellison's reaction was idiosyncratic or hyper-sensitive. We believe that a reasonable woman could have had a similar reaction. After receiving the first bizarre note from Gray, a person she barely knew, Ellison asked a co-worker to tell Gray to leave her alone. Despite her request, Gray sent her a long, passionate, disturbing letter. He told her he had been "watching" and "experiencing" her; he made repeated references to sex; he said he would write again. Ellison had no way of knowing what Gray would do next. A reasonable woman could consider Gray's conduct, as alleged by Ellison, sufficiently severe and pervasive to alter a condition of employment and create an abusive working environment.

---

13. If sexual comments or sexual advances are in fact welcomed by the recipient, they, of course, do not constitute sexual harassment. Title VII's prohibition of sex discrimination in employment does not require a totally desexualized work place.

Sexual harassment is a major problem in the workplace. Adopting the victim's perspective ensures that courts will not "sustain ingrained notions of reasonable behavior fashioned by the offenders." Congress did not enact Title VII to codify prevailing sexist prejudices. To the contrary, "Congress designed Title VII to prevent the perpetuation of stereotypes and a sense of degradation which serve to close or discourage employment opportunities for women." We hope that over time both men and women will learn what conduct offends reasonable members of the other sex. When employers and employees internalize the standard of workplace conduct we establish today, the current gap in perception between the sexes will be bridged.

IV

We next must determine what remedial actions by employers shield them from liability under Title VII for sexual harassment by co-workers. * * *

We ... believe that remedies should be "reasonably calculated to end the harassment." An employer's remedy should persuade individual harassers to discontinue unlawful conduct. We do not think that all harassment warrants dismissal; rather, remedies should be "assessed proportionately to the seriousness of the offense." Employers should impose sufficient penalties to assure a workplace free from sexual harassment. In essence, then, we think that the reasonableness of an employer's remedy will depend on its ability to stop harassment by the person who engaged in harassment.[17] In evaluating the adequacy of the remedy, the court may also take into account the remedy's ability to persuade potential harassers to refrain from unlawful conduct. Indeed, meting out punishments that do not take into account the need to maintain a harassment-free working environment may subject the employer to suit by the EEOC.

Here, Ellison's employer argues that it complied with its statutory obligation to provide a workplace free from sexual harassment. It promptly investigated Ellison's allegation. When Ellison returned to San Mateo from her training in St. Louis, Gray was no longer working in San Mateo. When Gray returned to San Mateo, the government granted Ellison's request to transfer temporarily to San Francisco.

We decline to accept the government's argument that its decision to return Gray to San Mateo did not create a hostile environment for Ellison because the government granted Ellison's request for a tempo-

---

17. We do not think that the appropriate inquiry is what a reasonable employer would do to remedy the sexual harassment. Although employers are statutorily obligated to provide a workplace free from sexual harassment, they may be reluctant, for business reasons, to punish high ranking and highly productive employees for sexual harassment. In addition, asking what a reasonable employer would do runs the risk of reinforcing any prevailing level of discrimination by employers and fails to focus directly on the best way to eliminate sexual harassment from the workplace.

rary transfer to San Francisco. Ellison preferred to work in San Mateo over San Francisco. We strongly believe that the victim of sexual harassment should not be punished for the conduct of the harasser. We wholeheartedly agree with the EEOC that a victim of sexual harassment should not have to work in a less desirable location as a result of an employer's remedy for sexual harassment.

Ellison maintains that the government's remedy was insufficient because it did not discipline Gray and because it allowed Gray to return to San Mateo after only a six-month separation. Even though the hostile environment had been eliminated when Gray began working in San Francisco, we cannot say that the government's response was reasonable under Title VII. The record on appeal suggests that Ellison's employer did not express strong disapproval of Gray's conduct, did not reprimand Gray, did not put him on probation, and did not inform him that repeated harassment would result in suspension or termination. Apparently, Gray's employer only told him to stop harassing Ellison. Title VII requires more than a mere request to refrain from discriminatory conduct. Employers send the wrong message to potential harassers when they do not discipline employees for sexual harassment. If Ellison can prove on remand that Gray knew or should have known that his conduct was unlawful and that the government failed to take even the mildest form of disciplinary action, the district court should hold that the government's initial remedy was insufficient under Title VII. At this point, genuine issues of material fact remain concerning whether the government properly disciplined Gray.

Ellison further maintains that her employer's decision to allow Gray to transfer back to the San Mateo office after a six-month cooling-off period rendered the government's remedy insufficient. She argues that Gray's *mere presence* would create a hostile working environment.

We believe that in some cases the mere presence of an employee who has engaged in particularly severe or pervasive harassment can create a hostile working environment. To avoid liability under Title VII for failing to remedy a hostile environment, employers may even have to remove employees from the workplace if their mere presence would render the working environment hostile. Once again, we examine whether the mere presence of a harasser would create a hostile environment from the perspective of a reasonable woman.

The district court did not reach the issue of the reasonableness of the government's remedy. Given the scant record on appeal, we cannot determine whether a reasonable woman could conclude that Gray's mere presence at San Mateo six months after the alleged harassment would create an abusive environment. Although we are aware of the severity of Gray's conduct (which we do not consider to be as serious as some other forms of harassment), we do not know how often Ellison and Gray would have to interact at San Mateo.

Moreover, it is not clear to us that the six-month cooling-off period was reasonably calculated to end the harassment or assessed proportionately to the seriousness of Gray's conduct. There is evidence in the record which suggests that the government intended to transfer Gray to San Francisco permanently and only allowed Gray to return to San Mateo because he promised to drop some union grievances. We do know that the IRS did not request Ellison's input or even inform her of the proceedings before agreeing to let Gray return to San Mateo. This failure to even attempt to determine what impact Gray's return would have on Ellison shows an insufficient regard for the victim's interest in avoiding a hostile working environment. On remand, the district court should fully explore the facts concerning the government's decision to return Gray to San Mateo.

V

We reverse the district court's decision that Ellison did not allege a prima facie case of sexual harassment due to a hostile working environment, and we remand for further proceedings consistent with this opinion. Although we have considered the evidence in the light most favorable to Ellison because the district court granted the government's motion for summary judgment, we, of course, reserve for the district court the resolution of all factual issues.

STEPHENS, DISTRICT JUDGE, dissenting:

This case comes to us on appeal in the wake of the granting of a summary judgment motion. There was no trial, therefore no opportunities for cross examination of the witnesses. In addition, there are factual gaps in the record that can only lead by speculation. Consequently, I believe that it is an inappropriate case with which to establish a new legal precedent which will be binding in all subsequent cases of like nature in the Ninth Circuit. I refer to the majority's use of the term "reasonable woman," a term I find ambiguous and therefore inadequate.

Nowhere in section 2000e of Title VII, the section under which the plaintiff in this case brought suit, is there any indication that Congress intended to provide for any other than equal treatment in the area of civil rights. The legislation is designed to achieve a balanced and generally gender neutral and harmonious workplace which would improve production and the quality of the employees' lives. In fact, the Supreme Court has shown a preference against systems that are not gender or race neutral, such as hiring quotas. While women may be the most frequent targets of this type of conduct that is at issue in this case, they are not the only targets. I believe that it is incumbent upon the court in this case to use terminology that will meet the needs of all who seek recourse under this section of Title VII. Possible alternatives that are more in line with a gender neutral approach include "victim," "target," or "person."

The term "reasonable man" as it is used in the law of torts, traditionally refers to the average adult person, regardless of gender, and the conduct that can reasonably be expected of him or her. For the purposes of the legal issues that are being addressed, such a term assumes that it is applicable to all persons. Section 2000e of Title VII presupposes the use of a legal term that can apply to all persons and the impossibility of a more individually tailored standard. It is clear that the authors of the majority opinion intend a difference between the "reasonable woman" and the "reasonable man" in Title VII cases on the assumption that men do not have the same sensibilities as women. This is not necessarily true. A man's response to circumstances faced by women and their effect upon women can be and in given circumstances may be expected to be understood by men.

It takes no stretch of the imagination to envision two complaints emanating from the same workplace regarding the same conditions, one brought by a woman and the other by a man. Application of the "new standard" presents a puzzlement which is born of the assumption that men's eyes do not see what a woman sees through her eyes. I find it surprising that the majority finds no need for evidence on any of these subjects. I am not sure whether the majority also concludes that the woman and the man in question are also reasonable without evidence on this subject. I am irresistibly drawn to the view that the conditions of the workplace itself should be examined as affected, among other things, by the conduct of the people working there as to whether the workplace as existing is conducive to fulfilling the goals of Title VII. In any event, these are unresolved factual issues which preclude summary judgment.

The focus on the victim of the sexually discriminatory conduct has its parallel in rape trials in the focus put by the defense on the victim's conduct rather than on the unlawful conduct of the person accused. Modern feminists have pointed out that concentration by the defense upon evidence concerning the background, appearance and conduct of women claiming to have been raped must be carefully controlled by the court to avoid effectively shifting the burden of proof to the victim. It is the accused, not the victim who is on trial, and it is therefore the conduct of the accused, not that of the victim, that should be subjected to scrutiny. Many state legislatures have responded to this viewpoint, and rules governing the presentation of evidence in rape cases have evolved accordingly.

It is my opinion that the case should be reversed with instructions to proceed to trial. This would certainly lead to filling in the factual gaps left by the scanty record, such as what happened at the time of or after the visit of Ellison to Gray's house to cause her to be subsequently fearful of his presence. The circumstances existing in the work place where only men are employed are different than they are where there are both male and female employees. The existence of the differences is readily recognizable and the conduct of employees can be changed appropriately. This is what Title VII requires. Whether a man or a woman has sensibilities peculiar to the person and what they are is not necessarily known. Until they become known by manifesting themselves in an obvious way, they do not become part of the circumstances of the work place. Consequently, the governing element in the equation is the workplace itself, not concepts or viewpoints of individual employees. This does not conflict with existing legal concepts.

The creation of the proposed "new standard" which applies only to women will not necessarily come to the aid of all potential victims of the type of misconduct that is at issue in this case. I believe that a gender neutral standard would greatly contribute to the clarity of this and future cases in the same area.

Summary judgment is not appropriate in this case.

Notes and Questions

1. Although the Ninth Circuit's decision in Ellison v. Brady has attracted much attention for its application of a "reasonable woman standard" in a Title VII sexual harassment case, this case was not the first to hold that the crucial issue is the perspective of the victim. See also Andrews v. City of Philadelphia, 895 F.2d 1469 (3d Cir.1990); Harris v. International Paper Co., 765 F.Supp. 1509 (D.Me.1991) (applying "reasonable black person standard," finding authority in earlier First Circuit case); Robinson v. Jacksonville Shipyards, Inc., 760 F.Supp. 1486 (M.D.Fla.1991); Barbetta v. Chemlawn Services Corp., 669 F.Supp. 569 (W.D.N.Y.1987).

2. Other courts continue to follow a "reasonable person" standard. In Rabidue v. Osceola Refining Co., 805 F.2d 611 (6th Cir.1986), cert. denied 481 U.S. 1041 (1987), the court held that the "trier of fact ... must adopt the perspective of a reasonable person's reaction to a similar environment under essentially like or similar circumstances." It is worth noting, however, that the Sixth Circuit seems a bit confused about the appropriate standard to apply in such cases. For instance, in Yates v. Avco Corp., 819 F.2d 630 (6th Cir.1987), the court applied a "reasonable woman" standard without refuting the holding of the Rabidue court. While citing to the dissent in Rabidue, the Yates court nonetheless included the employer's intent in its inquiry. Later Sixth Circuit cases, however, seem to ignore Yates. See, e.g., Dabish v. Chrysler Motors Corp., 902 F.2d 32 (6th Cir.1990) (citing Rabidue's holding). The Seventh Circuit has followed the Sixth Circuit in applying a "reasonable person" standard. See Scott v. Sears, Roebuck & Co.,

798 F.2d 210 (7th Cir.1986); Brooms v. Regal Tube Co., 881 F.2d 412 (7th Cir.1989).

3. Many courts seem unsure of which standard they are applying. For example, in Lipsett v. University of Puerto Rico, 864 F.2d 881 (1st Cir.1988), the court held that the trier of fact must look to the perspective of both the victim and the perpetrator. Citing to the dissent in *Rabidue,* however, the court's decision has been held to constitute an affirmance of the "reasonable woman" standard. Similarly, the Fifth Circuit's finding in Bennett v. Coroon & Black Corp., 845 F.2d 104 (5th Cir.1988), cert. denied 489 U.S. 1020 (1989), that "[a]ny reasonable person would have to consider these cartoons highly offensive to a woman ..." leaves open the question of whether this is truly an application of a "reasonable person" standard.

4. Another pervasive question is what kind of emphasis to place on obscene language and pornographic pictures. The tendency of courts using a "reasonable person" standard is to hold that such evidence alone will not constitute a hostile environment. According to the *Rabidue* court, "[t]he sexually oriented poster displays had a de minimis effect on the plaintiff's work environment when considered in the context of a society that condones and publicly features and commercially exploits open displays of written and pictorial erotica at the newsstands, on prime-time television, at the cinema, and in other public places." Thus, such courts emphasize overt propositions, offensive touching, and similarly persuasive evidence. Moreover, courts relying on the "reasonable person" standard consider whether the workplace in question was always a place of lewd language and obscene behavior. Thus, if these men had always put up pornographic pictures or used offensive language, then their conduct would not be discriminatory. ("the presence of actionable sexual harassment would be different depending upon the personality of the plaintiff and the prevailing work environment"). These courts seem therefore to incorporate a fault-based standard into Title VII.

5. One commentator has raised the question of whether a claim of hostile work environment, resulting from offensive speech alone, can withstand First Amendment arguments. Kingsley R. Browne, Title VII as Censorship: Hostile Environment and the First Amendment, 52 Ohio St.L.J. 481 (1991). Citing *Robinson,* as the first case to base liability on pictures and verbal abuse alone, Browne argues not only that such evidence is insufficient standing alone but also that evidence of such abuse should never be admissible. Do you agree?

3. PRIVACY

Page 518. Please add the following to note 5.

See also Mansfield v. American Telephone & Telegraph Co., 747 F.Supp. 1329 (W.D.Ark.1990) (claim for the tort of outrage stated where employer allegedly subjected the plaintiff to six hours of questioning, laughed at her and accused her of lying, accused her of having a lesbian relationship with a co-worker, and did not permit her to leave until she signed a statement).

Page 520. Please add the following after note 11.

11A. When an employee of the Grand Gulf Nuclear Power Station was hospitalized, rumors began to circulate that she was suffering from radiation exposure. To squelch these rumors, her co-workers were informed that the employee's illness was related to a recent hysterectomy. In an action for invasion of privacy, what result? See Young v. Jackson, 572 So.2d 378 (Miss.1990) (held: disclosure was privileged and therefore no liability).

4. FREEDOM OF EXPRESSION

Page 530. Please add the following after note 3.

3A. A bank teller refused to cash the state payroll check of a probationary corrections officer because the officer had no account with the bank. After the officer obtained authorization from a service representative, the teller cashed the check. As the officer was leaving the bank, from a distance of about 20 feet, the officer loudly said: "Hitler should have gotten rid of all you Jews." The teller was Egyptian. After the incident was reported to the officer's supervisor, he was discharged. He sued and argued that the discharge violated the First Amendment. What result? See Hawkins v. Department of Public Safety & Correctional Services, 325 Md. 621, 602 A.2d 712 (Ct.Spec.App.1992) (held: off-duty ethnic slur not a matter of public concern and therefore no duty to balance employee's interest against the state's interest in maintaining order in prison).

Page 531. Please add the following to note 5.

Does a municipal sick leave policy, which required sick employee to remain at home while recuperating from serious injury, violate the constitutional right to travel, right to consult with counsel, freedom of association, or right to vote? See Korenyi v. Department of Sanitation, 699 F.Supp. 388 (E.D.N.Y.1988) (held: no).

Page 531. Please add the following note.

8. A federal district court recently held that the Ethics Reform Act of 1989, in its prohibition on payments to federal executive branch employees for lawful outside activities such as giving speeches and writing articles, violated First Amendment guarantees. National Treasury Employees Union v. United States, 788 F.Supp. 4 (D.D.C.1992).

B. REGULATION OF OFF–WORK ACTIVITY

3. LIFESTYLE

Page 561. **Please add the following to note 3.**

Does it violate Title VII for a Catholic elementary school to refuse to renew the contract of a Protestant teacher because of her re-marriage? See Little v. Wuerl, 929 F.2d 944 (3d Cir.1991) (held: no).

Page 561. **Please add the following after note 4.**

4A. Does it violate the First Amendment for the IRS to suspend an attorney for five days for violating a rule requiring prior permission before engaging in outside practice, when he brought a class action against his church's board of directors for an accounting of church funds? See Williams v. IRS, 919 F.2d 745 (D.C.Cir.1990) (held: no).

C. SENIORITY AND PROMOTION

2. PROMOTIONS

Page 573. **Please add the following to note 2.**

Would it violate Title VII for an airline, in hiring pilots, to give a preference to the relatives of current employees? See Garland v. USAir, Inc., 767 F.Supp. 715 (W.D.Pa.1991) (held: yes). Compare this result with *Kotch,* p. 86.

Chapter 7

OCCUPATIONAL SAFETY AND HEALTH

A. INTRODUCTION

1. BACKGROUND

Page 586. Please add the following note.

4. The Omnibus Budget Reconciliation Act of 1990 increased the maximum penalties for willful and repeated violations from $10,000 to $70,000. Maximum penalties for serious, nonserious, failure to abate, and failure to post violations were increased from $1,000 to $7,000. Willful violations also now carry a minimum penalty of $5,000. The increases in penalties were designed to raise revenue—an estimated $900 million in the first five years according to the Congressional Budget Office.

2. JURISDICTION

Page 601. Please add the following note.

4. On remand, after an eight-month bench trial, the defendants were acquitted on the charges of aggravated battery, reckless conduct, and conspiracy. The court found that the defendants knew of the hazardous substances in the plant and the poor working conditions, but the state failed to prove beyond a reasonable doubt that workers' ailments were caused by conditions at the plant. The court also found inadequate evidence of reckless conduct or conspiracy.

E. ENFORCEMENT AND ADJUDICATION

2. ADJUDICATORY PROCESS

Page 680. Before part "F" please add the following.

Note

In Martin v. OSHRC, 111 S.Ct. 1171 (1991), the Supreme Court held that in judicial review of a contested citation, when the Secretary and the Commission both have reasonable but conflicting interpretations of an ambiguous standard, the reviewing court should defer to the Secretary's interpretation.

G. NON–OSHA SAFETY AND HEALTH LAW

3. ANTI–DISCRIMINATION LAWS

Page 692. Please omit the main case and replace it with the following.

INTERNATIONAL UNION, UAW v. JOHNSON CONTROLS, INC.
111 S.Ct. 1196 (1991).

JUSTICE BLACKMUN delivered the opinion of the Court.

In this case we are concerned with an employer's gender-based fetal-protection policy. May an employer exclude a fertile female employee from certain jobs because of its concern for the health of the fetus the woman might conceive?

I

Respondent Johnson Controls, Inc., manufactures batteries. In the manufacturing process, the element lead is a primary ingredient. Occupational exposure to lead entails health risks, including the risk of harm to any fetus carried by a female employee.

Before the Civil Rights Act of 1964 became law, Johnson Controls did not employ any woman in a battery-manufacturing job. In June 1977, however, it announced its first official policy concerning its employment of women in lead-exposure work:

> "[P]rotection of the health of the unborn child is the immediate and direct responsibility of the prospective parents. While the medical profession and the company can support them in the exercise of this responsibility, it cannot assume it for them without simultaneously infringing their rights as persons.

> · · · · ·

>   ".... Since not all women who can become mothers wish to become mothers (or will become mothers), it would appear to be illegal discrimination to treat all who are capable of pregnancy as though they will become pregnant."

Consistent with that view, Johnson Controls "stopped short of excluding women capable of bearing children from lead exposure," but emphasized that a woman who expected to have a child should not choose a job in which she would have such exposure. The company also required a woman who wished to be considered for employment to sign a statement that she had been advised of the risk of having a child while she was exposed to lead. The statement informed the woman that although there was evidence "that women exposed to lead have a higher rate of abortion," this evidence was "not as clear ... as the relationship between cigarette smoking and cancer," but that it was, "medically speaking, just good sense not to run that risk if you want children and do not want to expose the unborn child to risk, however small...."

Five years later, in 1982, Johnson Controls shifted from a policy of warning to a policy of exclusion. Between 1979 and 1983, eight employees became pregnant while maintaining blood lead levels in excess of 30 micrograms per deciliter. This appeared to be the critical level noted by the Occupational Health and Safety Administration (OSHA) for a worker who was planning to have a family. The company responded by announcing a broad exclusion of women from jobs that exposed them to lead:

> "... [I]t is [Johnson Controls'] policy that women who are pregnant or who are capable of bearing children will not be placed into jobs involving lead exposure or which could expose them to lead through the exercise of job bidding, bumping, transfer or promotion rights."

The policy defined "women ... capable of bearing children" as "[a]ll women except those whose inability to bear children is medically documented." It further stated that an unacceptable work station was one where, "over the past year," an employee had recorded a blood lead level of more than 30 micrograms per deciliter or the work site had yielded an air sample containing a lead level in excess of 30 micrograms per cubic meter.

II

In April 1984, petitioners filed in the United States District Court for the Eastern District of Wisconsin a class action challenging Johnson Controls' fetal-protection policy as sex discrimination that violated Title VII of the Civil Rights Act of 1964, as amended. Among the individual plaintiffs were petitioners Mary Craig, who had chosen to be sterilized in order to avoid losing her job, Elsie Nason, a 50–year–old divorcee, who had suffered a loss in compensation when she was transferred out of a job where she was exposed to lead, and Donald Penney, who had been denied a request for a leave of absence for the purpose of lowering his lead level because he intended to become a father. Upon stipulation of the parties, the District Court certified a class consisting of "all past, present and future production and maintenance employees" in United Auto Workers bargaining units at nine of Johnson Controls' plants "who have been and continue to be affected by [the employer's] Fetal Protection Policy implemented in 1982."

The District Court granted summary judgment for defendant-respondent Johnson Controls. Applying a three-part business necessity defense derived from fetal-protection cases in the Courts of Appeals for the Fourth and Eleventh Circuits, the District Court concluded that while "there is a disagreement among the experts regarding the effect of lead on the fetus," the hazard to the fetus through exposure to lead was established by "a considerable body of opinion"; that although "[e]xpert opinion has been provided which holds that lead also affects the reproductive abilities of men and women ... [and] that these effects are as great as the effects of exposure of the fetus ... a great body of experts are of the opinion that the fetus is more vulnerable to levels of lead that would not affect adults"; and that petitioners had "failed to establish that there is an acceptable alternative policy which would protect the fetus." The court stated that, in view of this disposition of the business necessity defense, it did not "have to undertake a bona fide occupational qualification's (BFOQ) analysis."

The Court of Appeals for the Seventh Circuit, sitting en banc, affirmed the summary judgment by a 7–to–4 vote. The majority held that the proper standard for evaluating the fetal-protection policy was the defense of business necessity; that Johnson Controls was entitled to summary judgment under that defense; and that even if the proper standard was a BFOQ, Johnson Controls still was entitled to summary judgment.

The Court of Appeals first reviewed fetal-protection opinions from the Eleventh and Fourth Circuits. See Hayes v. Shelby Memorial Hospital, 726 F.2d 1543 (CA11 1984), and Wright v. Olin Corp., 697 F.2d 1172 (CA4 1982). Those opinions established the three-step business necessity inquiry: whether there is a substantial health risk to the fetus; whether transmission of the hazard to the fetus occurs only through women; and whether there is a less discriminatory alternative equally capable of preventing the health hazard to the fetus. The Court of Appeals agreed with the Eleventh and Fourth Circuits that "the components of the business necessity defense the courts of appeals and the EEOC have utilized in fetal protection cases balance the interests of the employer, the employee and the unborn child in a manner consistent with Title VII."

* * *

III

The bias in Johnson Controls' policy is obvious. Fertile men, but not fertile women, are given a choice as to whether they wish to risk their reproductive health for a particular job. Section 703(a) of the Civil Rights Act of 1964 prohibits sex-based classifications in terms and conditions of employment, in hiring and discharging decisions, and in other employment decisions that adversely affect an employee's status. Respondent's fetal-protection policy explicitly discriminates against women on the basis of their sex. The policy excludes women with childbearing capacity from lead-exposed jobs and so creates a facial classification based on gender. Respondent assumes as much in its brief before this Court.

Nevertheless, the Court of Appeals assumed, as did the two appellate courts who already had confronted the issue, that sex-specific fetal-protection policies do not involve facial discrimination. These courts analyzed the policies as though they were facially neutral, and had only a discriminatory effect upon the employment opportunities of women. Consequently, the courts looked to see if each employer in question had established that its policy was justified as a business necessity. The business necessity standard is more lenient for the employer than the statutory BFOQ defense. The Court of Appeals here went one step further and invoked the burden-shifting framework set forth in Wards Cove Packing Co. v. Atonio, 490 U.S. 642 (1989), thus requiring petitioners to bear the burden of persuasion on all questions. The court assumed that because the asserted reason for the sex-based exclusion (protecting women's unconceived offspring) was ostensibly benign, the policy was not sex-based discrimination. That assumption, however, was incorrect.

First, Johnson Controls' policy classifies on the basis of gender and childbearing capacity, rather than fertility alone. Respondent does not seek to protect the unconceived children of all its employees. Despite evidence in the record about the debilitating effect of lead exposure on the male reproductive system, Johnson Controls is concerned only with the harms that may befall the unborn offspring of its female employees. Accordingly, it appears that Johnson Controls would have lost in the Eleventh Circuit under Hayes because its policy does not "effectively and equally protec[t] the offspring of all employees." This Court faced a conceptually similar situation in Phillips v. Martin Marietta Corp., 400 U.S. 542 (1971), and found sex discrimination because the policy established "one hiring policy for women and another for men—each having pre-school-age children." Johnson Controls' policy is facially discriminatory because it requires only a female employee to produce proof that she is not capable of reproducing.

Our conclusion is bolstered by the Pregnancy Discrimination Act of 1978 (PDA), 92 Stat. 2076, 42 U.S.C. § 2000e(k), in which Congress explicitly provided that, for purposes of Title VII, discrimination "on the basis of sex" includes discrimination "because of or on the basis of pregnancy, childbirth, or related medical conditions."[3] "The Pregnancy Discrimination Act has now made clear that, for all Title VII purposes, discrimination based on a woman's pregnancy is, on its face, discrimination because of her sex." In its use of the words "capable of bearing children" in the 1982 policy statement as the criterion for

---

3. The Act added subsection (k) to § 701 of the Civil Rights Act of 1964 and reads in pertinent part:

"The terms 'because of sex' or 'on the basis of sex' (in Title VII) include, but are not limited to, because of or on the basis of pregnancy, childbirth, or related medical conditions; and women affected by pregnancy, childbirth, or related medical conditions shall be treated the same for all employment-related purposes as other persons not so affected but similar in their ability or inability to work...."

exclusion, Johnson Controls explicitly classifies on the basis of potential for pregnancy. Under the PDA, such a classification must be regarded, for Title VII purposes, in the same light as explicit sex discrimination. Respondent has chosen to treat all its female employees as potentially pregnant; that choice evinces discrimination on the basis of sex.

We concluded above that Johnson Controls' policy is not neutral because it does not apply to the reproductive capacity of the company's male employees in the same way as it applies to that of the females. Moreover, the absence of a malevolent motive does not convert a facially discriminatory policy into a neutral policy with a discriminatory effect. Whether an employment practice involves disparate treatment through explicit facial discrimination does not depend on why the employer discriminates but rather on the explicit terms of the discrimination.

* * *

In sum, Johnson Controls' policy "does not pass the simple test of whether the evidence shows 'treatment of a person in a manner which but for that person's sex would be different.'" We hold that Johnson Controls' fetal-protection policy is sex discrimination forbidden under Title VII unless respondent can establish that sex is a "bona fide occupational qualification."

IV

Under § 703(e)(1) of Title VII, an employer may discriminate on the basis of "religion, sex, or national origin in those certain instances where religion, sex, or national origin is a bona fide occupational qualification reasonably necessary to the normal operation of that particular business or enterprise." We therefore turn to the question whether Johnson Controls' fetal-protection policy is one of those "certain instances" that come within the BFOQ exception.

The BFOQ defense is written narrowly, and this Court has read it narrowly. Our emphasis on the restrictive scope of the BFOQ defense is grounded on both the language and the legislative history of § 703.

* * *

Johnson Controls argues that its fetal-protection policy falls within the so-called safety exception to the BFOQ. Our cases have stressed that discrimination on the basis of sex because of safety concerns is allowed only in narrow circumstances. In Dothard v. Rawlinson, 433 U.S. 321 (1977), this Court indicated that danger to a woman herself does not justify discrimination. We there allowed the employer to hire only male guards in contact areas of maximum-security male penitentiaries only because more was at stake than the "individual woman's decision to weigh and accept the risks of employment." We found sex to be a BFOQ inasmuch as the employment of a female guard would create real risks of safety to others if violence broke out because the guard was a woman. Sex discrimination was tolerated because sex was related to the guard's ability to do the job—maintaining prison security. We also required in *Dothard* a high correlation between sex and ability to perform job functions and refused to allow employers to use sex as a proxy for strength although it might be a fairly accurate one.

Similarly, some courts have approved airlines' layoffs of pregnant flight attendants at different points during the first five months of pregnancy on the ground that the employer's policy was necessary to ensure the safety of passengers. In two of these cases, the courts pointedly indicated that fetal, as opposed to passenger, safety was best left to the mother.

We considered safety to third parties in Western Airlines, Inc. v. Criswell, 472 U.S. 400 (1985), in the context of the ADEA. We focused upon "the nature of the flight engineer's tasks," and the "actual capabilities of persons over age 60" in relation to those tasks. Our safety concerns were not independent of the individual's ability to perform the assigned tasks, but rather involved the possibility that, because of age-connected debility, a flight engineer might not properly assist the pilot, and might thereby cause a safety emergency. Furthermore, although we considered the safety of third parties in *Dothard* and *Criswell*, those third parties were indispensable to the particular business at issue. In *Dothard,* the third parties were the inmates; in *Criswell,* the third parties were the passengers on the plane. We stressed that in order to qualify as a BFOQ, a job qualification must relate to the "essence," or to the "central mission of the employer's business."

The concurrence ignores the "essence of the business" test and so concludes that "the safety to fetuses in carrying out the duties of battery manufacturing is as much a legitimate concern as is safety to third parties in guarding prisons (*Dothard*) or flying airplanes (*Criswell*)." By limiting its discussion to cost and safety concerns and rejecting the "essence of the business" test that our case law has established, the concurrence seeks to expand what is now the narrow BFOQ defense. Third-party safety considerations properly entered into the BFOQ analysis in *Dothard* and *Criswell* because they went to the core of the employee's job performance. Moreover, that performance involved the central purpose of the enterprise. *Dothard* ("The essence of a correctional counselor's job is to maintain prison security"); *Criswell* (the central mission of the airline's business was the safe transportation of its passengers). The concurrence attempts to transform this case into one of customer safety. The unconceived fetuses of Johnson Controls' female employees, however, are neither customers nor third parties whose safety is essential to the business of battery manufacturing. No one can disregard the possibility of injury to future children;

the BFOQ, however, is not so broad that it transforms this deep social concern into an essential aspect of batterymaking.

Our case law, therefore, makes clear that the safety exception is limited to instances in which sex or pregnancy actually interferes with the employee's ability to perform the job. This approach is consistent with the language of the BFOQ provision itself, for it suggests that permissible distinctions based on sex must relate to ability to perform the duties of the job. Johnson Controls suggests, however, that we expand the exception to allow fetal-protection policies that mandate particular standards for pregnant or fertile women. We decline to do so. Such an expansion contradicts not only the language of the BFOQ and the narrowness of its exception but the plain language and history of the Pregnancy Discrimination Act.

The PDA's amendment to Title VII contains a BFOQ standard of its own: unless pregnant employees differ from others "in their ability or inability to work," they must be "treated the same" as other employees "for all employment-related purposes." This language clearly sets forth Congress' remedy for discrimination on the basis of pregnancy and potential pregnancy. Women who are either pregnant or potentially pregnant must be treated like others "similar in their ability ... to work." In other words, women as capable of doing their jobs as their male counterparts may not be forced to choose between having a child and having a job.

The concurrence asserts that the PDA did not alter the BFOQ defense. The concurrence arrives at this conclusion by ignoring the second clause of the Act which states that "women affected by pregnancy, childbirth, or related medical conditions shall be treated the same for all employment-related purposes ... as other persons not so affected but similar in their ability or inability to work." Until this day, every Member of this Court had acknowledged that "[t]he second clause [of the PDA] could not be clearer: it mandates that pregnant employees 'shall be treated the same for all employment-related purposes' as nonpregnant employees similarly situated with respect to their ability or inability to work." The concurrence now seeks to read the second clause out of the Act.

The legislative history confirms what the language of the Pregnancy Discrimination Act compels. Both the House and Senate Reports accompanying the legislation indicate that this statutory standard was chosen to protect female workers from being treated differently from other employees simply because of their capacity to bear children.

* * *

This history counsels against expanding the BFOQ to allow fetal-protection policies. The Senate Report quoted above states that employers may not require a pregnant woman to stop working at any time during her pregnancy unless she is unable to do her work. Employment late in pregnancy often imposes risks on the unborn child, but Congress indicated that the employer may take into account only the woman's ability to get her job done. With the PDA, Congress made clear that the decision to become pregnant or to work while being either pregnant or capable of becoming pregnant was reserved for each individual woman to make for herself.

We conclude that the language of both the BFOQ provision and the PDA which amended it, as well as the legislative history and the case law, prohibit an employer from discriminating against a woman because of her capacity to become pregnant unless her reproductive potential prevents her from performing the duties of her job. We reiterate our holdings in *Criswell* and *Dothard* that an employer must direct its concerns about a woman's ability to perform her job safely and efficiently to those aspects of the woman's job-related activities that fall within the "essence" of the particular business.

V

We have no difficulty concluding that Johnson Controls cannot establish a BFOQ. Fertile women, as far as appears in the record, participate in the manufacture of batteries as efficiently as anyone else. Johnson Controls' professed moral and ethical concerns about the welfare of the next generation do not suffice to establish a BFOQ of female sterility. Decisions about the welfare of future children must be left to the parents who conceive, bear, support, and raise them rather than to the employers who hire those parents. Congress has mandated this choice through Title VII, as amended by the Pregnancy Discrimination Act. Johnson Controls has attempted to exclude women because of their reproductive capacity. Title VII and the PDA simply do not allow a woman's dismissal because of her failure to submit to sterilization.

Nor can concerns about the welfare of the next generation be considered a part of the "essence" of Johnson Controls' business. Judge Easterbrook in this case pertinently observed: "It is word play to say that 'the job' at Johnson [Controls] is to make batteries without risk to fetuses in the same way 'the job' at Western Air Lines is to fly planes without crashing."

Johnson Controls argues that it must exclude all fertile women because it is impossible to tell which women will become pregnant while working with lead. This argument is somewhat academic in light of our conclusion that the company may not exclude fertile women at all; it perhaps is worth noting, however, that Johnson Controls has shown no "factual basis for believing that all or substantially all women would be unable to perform safely and efficiently the duties of the job involved." Even on this sparse record, it is apparent that Johnson Controls is concerned about only a small minority of women.

Of the eight pregnancies reported among the female employees, it has not been shown that any of the babies have birth defects or other abnormalities. The record does not reveal the birth rate for Johnson Controls' female workers but national statistics show that approximately nine percent of all fertile women become pregnant each year. The birthrate drops to two percent for blue collar workers over age 30. Johnson Controls' fear of prenatal injury, no matter how sincere, does not begin to show that substantially all of its fertile women employees are incapable of doing their jobs.

VI

A word about tort liability and the increased cost of fertile women in the workplace is perhaps necessary. One of the dissenting judges in this case expressed concern about an employer's tort liability and concluded that liability for a potential injury to a fetus is a social cost that Title VII does not require a company to ignore. It is correct to say that Title VII does not prevent the employer from having a conscience. The statute, however, does prevent sex-specific fetal-protection policies. These two aspects of Title VII do not conflict.

More than 40 States currently recognize a right to recover for a prenatal injury based either on negligence or on wrongful death. According to Johnson Controls, however, the company complies with the lead standard developed by OSHA and warns its female employees about the damaging effects of lead. It is worth noting that OSHA gave the problem of lead lengthy consideration and concluded that "there is no basis whatsoever for the claim that women of childbearing age should be excluded from the workplace in order to protect the fetus or the course of pregnancy." Instead, OSHA established a series of mandatory protections which, taken together, "should effectively minimize any risk to the fetus and newborn child." Without negligence, it would be difficult for a court to find liability on the part of the employer. If, under general tort principles, Title VII bans sex-specific fetal-protection policies, the employer fully informs the woman of the risk, and the employer has not acted negligently, the basis for holding an employer liable seems remote at best.

Although the issue is not before us, the concurrence observes that "it is far from clear that compliance with Title VII will preempt state tort liability."

* * *

If state tort law furthers discrimination in the workplace and prevents employers from hiring women who are capable of manufacturing the product as efficiently as men, then it will impede the accomplishment of Congress' goals in enacting Title VII. Because Johnson Controls has not argued that it faces any costs from tort liability, not to mention crippling ones, the pre-emption question is not before us. We therefore say no more than that the concurrence's speculation appears unfounded as well as premature.

The tort-liability argument reduces to two equally unpersuasive propositions. First, Johnson Controls attempts to solve the problem of reproductive health hazards by resorting to an exclusionary policy. Title VII plainly forbids illegal sex discrimination as a method of diverting attention from an employer's obligation to police the workplace. Second, the spectre of an award of damages reflects a fear that hiring fertile women will cost more. The extra cost of employing members of one sex, however, does not provide an affirmative Title VII defense for a discriminatory refusal to hire members of that gender. Indeed, in passing the PDA, Congress considered at length the considerable cost of providing equal treatment of pregnancy and related conditions, but made the "decision to forbid special treatment of pregnancy despite the social costs associated therewith."

We, of course, are not presented with, nor do we decide, a case in which costs would be so prohibitive as to threaten the survival of the employer's business. We merely reiterate our prior holdings that the incremental cost of hiring women cannot justify discriminating against them.

VII

Our holding today that Title VII, as so amended, forbids sex-specific fetal-protection policies is neither remarkable nor unprecedented. Concern for a woman's existing or potential offspring historically has been the excuse for denying women equal employment opportunities. Congress in the PDA prohibited discrimination on the basis of a woman's ability to become pregnant. We do no more than hold that the Pregnancy Discrimination Act means what it says.

It is no more appropriate for the courts than it is for individual employers to decide whether a woman's reproductive role is more important to herself and her family than her economic role. Congress has left this choice to the woman as hers to make.

The judgment of the Court of Appeals is reversed and the case is remanded for further proceedings consistent with this opinion.

It is so ordered.

JUSTICE WHITE, with whom THE CHIEF JUSTICE and JUSTICE KENNEDY join, concurring in part and concurring in the judgment.

The Court properly holds that Johnson Controls' fetal protection policy overtly discriminates against women, and thus is prohibited by Title VII unless it falls within the bona fide occupational qualification (BFOQ) exception, set forth at 42 U.S.C. § 2000e–2(e). The Court erroneously holds, however, that the BFOQ defense is so narrow that it could never justify a sex-specific fetal protection policy. I nevertheless concur in the judgment of reversal because on the record before us summary judgment in favor of Johnson Controls was improperly entered by the District Court and affirmed by the Court of Appeals.

* * *

The Court dismisses the possibility of tort liability by no more than speculating that if "Title VII bans sex-specific fetal-protection policies, the employer fully informs the woman of the risk, and the employer has not acted negligently, the basis for holding an employer liable seems remote at best." Such speculation will be small comfort to employers. First, it is far from clear that compliance with Title VII will pre-empt state tort liability, and the Court offers no support for that proposition. Second, although warnings may preclude claims by injured *employees,* they will not preclude claims by injured children because the general rule is that parents cannot waive causes of action on behalf of their children, and the parents' negligence will not be imputed to the children. Finally, although state tort liability for prenatal injuries generally requires negligence, it will be difficult for employers to determine in advance what will constitute negligence. Compliance with OSHA standards, for example, has been held not to be a defense to state tort or criminal liability. Moreover, it is possible that employers will be held strictly liable, if, for example, their manufacturing process is considered "abnormally dangerous."

Relying on Los Angeles Dept. of Water and Power v. Manhart, 435 U.S. 702 (1978), the Court contends that tort liability cannot justify a fetal protection policy because the extra costs of hiring women is not a defense under Title VII. This contention misrepresents our decision in *Manhart.* There, we held that a requirement that female employees contribute more than male employees to a pension fund, in order to reflect the greater longevity of women, constituted discrimination against women under Title VII because it treated them as a class rather than as individuals. We did not in that case address in any detail the nature of the BFOQ defense, and we certainly did not hold that cost was irrelevant to the BFOQ analysis. Rather, we merely stated in a footnote that "there has been no showing that sex distinctions are reasonably necessary to the normal operation of the Department's retirement plan." We further noted that although Title VII does not contain a "cost-justification defense comparable to the affirmative defense available in a price discrimination suit," "no defense based on the *total* cost of employing men and women was attempted in this case."

* * *

JUSTICE SCALIA, concurring in the judgment.

I generally agree with the Court's analysis, but have some reservations, several of which bear mention.

First, I think it irrelevant that there was "evidence in the record about the debilitating effect of lead exposure on the male reproductive system." Even without such evidence, treating women differently "on the basis of pregnancy" constitutes discrimination "on the basis of sex," because Congress has unequivocally said so.

Second, the Court points out that "Johnson Controls has shown no factual basis for believing that all or substantially all women would be unable to perform safely ... the duties of the job involved," (internal quotations omitted). In my view, this is not only "somewhat academic in light of our conclusion that the company may not exclude fertile women at all," *ibid.;* it is entirely irrelevant. By reason of the Pregnancy Discrimination Act, it would not matter if all pregnant women placed their children at risk in taking these jobs, just as it does not matter if no men do so. As Judge Easterbrook put it in his dissent below, "Title VII gives parents the power to make occupational decisions affecting their families. A legislative forum is available to those who believe that such decisions should be made elsewhere."

Third, I am willing to assume, as the Court intimates, that any action required by Title VII cannot give rise to liability under state tort law. That assumption, however, does not answer the question whether an action *is* required by Title VII (including the BFOQ provision) even if it is subject to liability under state tort law. It is perfectly reasonable to believe that Title VII has *accommodated* state tort law through the BFOQ exception. However, all that need be said in the present case is that Johnson has not demonstrated a substantial risk of tort liability—which is alone enough to defeat a tort-based assertion of the BFOQ exception.

Notes and Questions

1. Based on the majority opinion, would it violate Title VII for a hospital to require that already-pregnant x-ray technicians be reassigned to other jobs in the hospital for the duration of their pregnancy?

2. Justice Blackmun's opinion relies on the principle of autonomy.

The bias in Johnson Controls' policy is obvious. Fertile men, but not fertile women, are given a choice as to whether they wish to risk their reproductive health for a particular job.

To what extent should decisions about risk acceptability be left to employees? Does OSHA rely on autonomy or paternalism? What about the Americans with Disabilities Act?

3. How reassured are employers likely to be that their potential tort liability is "remote at best"? How would you address the issue of possible tort liability?

Chapter 8

DISABLING INJURY AND ILLNESS

A. WORKERS' COMPENSATION

2. COVERAGE

Page 723. Please add the following note.

11. A waitress sued the owner of the restaurant to recover for salmonella poisoning she contracted as a result of eating a discount meal before beginning her shift. Is the action barred by workers' compensation? See Pagani v. BT II, Ltd. Partnership, 24 Conn.App. 739, 592 A.2d 397 (1991), appeal dismissed 220 Conn. 902, 593 A.2d 968 (1991) (held: no).

3. OCCUPATIONAL DISEASE

Page 731. Please add the following to note 1.

Cf. Stiles v. Royal Insurance Co. of America, 798 S.W.2d 591 (Tex.App. 1990) (insufficient evidence that heart attack of pizza parlor employee was work related).

6. TORT ACTIONS AND "EXCLUSIVITY"

Page 754. Please add the following to note 3.

An employee who was injured when attacked by her employer's dog in the course of her employment sued her employer in his dual capacity as dog owner. Has she stated a cognizable exception to the exclusive remedy rule? See Barrett v. Rodgers, 408 Mass. 614, 562 N.E.2d 480 (1990) (held: no).

Page 754. Please add the following note.

7. In Collins v. City of Harker Heights, 112 S.Ct. 1061 (1992), the Supreme Court held that the estate of a municipal employee who was fatally injured in the course of employment because of the city's failure to warn its employees about known hazards in the workplace did not have a remedy under 42 U.S.C. § 1983.

Part IV

TERMINATING THE RELATIONSHIP

Chapter 9

LEAVING A JOB

B. PROMISES NOT TO COMPETE

Page 813. Please add the following to note 3.

See also Hill v. Mobile Auto Trim, Inc., 725 S.W.2d 168 (Tex.1987) (lack of consideration for agreement not to compete when the franchisee had acquired his skills before signing franchise agreement).

Should noncompetition agreements designed to limit employment in a "common calling" be enforced? The court in *Hill* held that such agreements are not enforceable. See also Appalachian Laboratories, Inc. v. Bostic, 178 W.Va. 386, 359 S.E.2d 614 (1987) (no protected employer interest in enforcement of restrictive agreement against employee who had only general managerial skills and knowledge).

Page 814. Please add the following note.

6. A Texas court held that, despite a contractual provision making Florida law the governing law, it would apply Texas law to an agreement not to compete because Florida law was "contrary to the fundamental public policy of Texas." The court then found the noncompetition agreement unenforceable. DeSantis v. Wackenhut Corp., 793 S.W.2d 670 (Tex.1990).

Page 822. Please add the following note.

11. A California court upheld an injunction issued to restrain KGB radio's former employee—the "chicken man"—from appearing anywhere in the station's chicken costume which bore the station's trademark on the vest. The court struck down, however, the preliminary injunction forbidding the former employee from appearing in a "substantially similar" chicken suit as an invalid restriction on Giannoulas' "right to earn a living and to express himself as an artist." KGB, Inc. v. Giannoulas, 104 Cal.App.3d 844, 164 Cal.Rptr. 571 (1980).

C. TRADE SECRETS

Page 832. Please add the following to the end of note 3.

In B.C. Ziegler & Co. v. Ehren, 141 Wis.2d 19, 414 N.W.2d 48 (Ct.App. 1987), the court permanently enjoined a purchaser of scrap paper which contained customer information inadvertently disclosed by a securities underwriter from using the information. According to the court, the trade secret status of the information survives inadvertent disclosure.

Page 835. Please add the following to note (c).

Moss, Adams, & Co. was distinguished by a California court which found that a former employee's letter went beyond an announcement of new employment and became a solicitation of customers. American Credit Indemnity Co. v. Sacks, 213 Cal.App.3d 622, 262 Cal.Rptr. 92 (1989).

Page 838. Please add the following note.

16.   See Pat K. Chew, Competing Interests in the Corporate Opportunity Doctrine, 67 N.C.L.Rev. 435 (1989). Professor Chew argues that courts should give more protection to the interests of fiduciary employees by using a reasonable expectation test to evaluate claims that a fiduciary has violated the fiduciary duty by pursuing a business opportunity that a former corporate employer claims belonged to the entity. Currently, she contends, courts give too much weight to the corporate interest to the detriment of rights of individual employees.

> [T]he practical consequences for corporate fiduciaries are drastic. In many instances fiduciaries who lose corporate opportunity lawsuits are effectively prohibited from competing with their former corporations. This results even though the fiduciaries have not signed noncompetition agreements. Such de facto restraints are contrary to individuals' rights to pursue freely their interests and talents and to society's long-standing goal of promoting competition.

Id. at 438. In Allied Supply Co. v. Brown, 585 So.2d 33 (Ala.1991), the Alabama Supreme Court held that at-will employees do not breach a fiduciary duty by failing to give their employer advance notice of resignation before forming a new business.

Chapter 10

DISCHARGE

B. JUDICIAL EROSION OF EMPLOYMENT AT WILL

1. THE PUBLIC POLICY EXCEPTION TO THE AT WILL RULE

Page 847. Please omit the main case and replace it with the following two cases.

GANTT v. SENTRY INSURANCE
1 Cal.4th 1083, 4 Cal.Rptr.2d 874, 824 P.2d 680 (1992).

ARABIAN, JUSTICE.

We granted review in this case to consider whether an employee who was terminated in retaliation for supporting a coworker's claim of sexual harassment may state a cause of action for tortious discharge against public policy and, if so, whether the exclusive remedy provisions of the Workers' Compensation Act bar the action. We hold that the claim is actionable under Tameny v. Atlantic Richfield Co. (1980) 27 Cal.3d 167, 164 Cal.Rptr. 839, 610 P.2d 1330 (*Tameny*), and is not preempted by the workers' compensation law.

I. PROCEDURAL BACKGROUND

Defendants, Sentry Insurance (Sentry), Frank Singer (Singer) and Caroline Fribance (Fribance) appealed from a judgment entered on a jury verdict of $1.34 million in favor of plaintiff, Vincent A. Gantt (hereafter plaintiff or Gantt) in his action for tortious discharge in violation of the covenant of good faith and fair dealing and in contravention of public policy, defamation, and intentional infliction of emotional distress.

The Court of Appeal reversed the judgment as to the individual defendants but affirmed in all other respects. As to the *Tameny* cause of action, the Court of Appeal noted that the allegation was predicated upon two distinct theories: the first, that plaintiff was constructively discharged in retaliation for supporting a coworker's claim of sexual harassment; and second, that Sentry attempted to induce plaintiff to give false information or to withhold information from the public agency investigating the sexual harassment charges. Although the Court of Appeal concluded that Gantt's first theory of recovery was preempted by the California Fair Employment and Housing Act (FEHA), it held that the FEHA did not preempt a *Tameny* claim

73

premised on the second theory; that substantial evidence supported the jury's special verdict; and that the action was not barred by the exclusive remedy provisions of the Workers' Compensation Act.[1]

Sentry petitioned this court for review, asserting that neither the facts nor the law supported a *Tameny* claim premised on plaintiff's second theory, and that the action was barred in any event by the workers' compensation law. After granting review, we requested additional briefing on the question whether a *Tameny* claim must be grounded in a violation of statute or constitutional provision.[2]

For the reasons set forth below, we conclude that a termination in retaliation for testifying truthfully concerning a coworker's sexual harassment claim in the context of an administrative investigation is actionable under *Tameny*. We further conclude that neither the FEHA nor the Workers' Compensation Act preempts the claim. Accordingly, we shall affirm the decision of the Court of Appeal.

II. FACTS

Viewing the record most strongly in favor of the judgment, as we must, the following pertinent chronology of facts appears: In September 1979, Sentry hired Gantt to serve as the sales manager of its Sacramento office. His mission was to develop the Sacramento sales force. How successfully he performed this task was the subject of conflicting evidence at trial. However, as explained below, the record amply supports the jury's specific finding that his demotion and constructive discharge were the product of his support for another employee's sexual harassment claim rather than the result of any legally valid business reason.

The specific circumstances which led to Gantt's estrangement from Sentry centered on Joyce Bruno, who was hired in January 1980 to be the liaison between trade associations and Sentry's Sacramento and

---

1. With respect to Gantt's other causes of action, the Court of Appeal held that the tort claim for breach of the covenant of good faith and fair dealing was invalid under this court's decisions in Foley v. Interactive Data Corp. (1988) 47 Cal.3d 654, 254 Cal.Rptr. 211, 765 P.2d 373 and Newman v. Emerson Radio Corp. (1989) 48 Cal.3d 973, 258 Cal.Rptr. 592, 772 P.2d 1059; that the intentional infliction of emotional distress claim was barred by the exclusive remedy provisions of the workers' compensation law as construed by this court in Cole v. Fair Oaks Fire Protection Dist. (1987) 43 Cal.3d 148, 233 Cal.Rptr. 308, 729 P.2d 743; and that the defamation action was precluded because of the privileged nature of the statements at issue. Because plaintiff sought recovery against the individual defendants (Singer and Fribance) solely on the grounds of defamation and intentional infliction of emotional distress, the Court of Appeal reversed the judgment as to them. Gantt did not seek review of these portions of the Court of Appeal's decision.

2. We also requested additional briefing on the question whether, in light of our intervening decision in Rojo v. Kliger (1990) 52 Cal.3d 65, 276 Cal.Rptr. 130, 801 P.2d 373, the Court of Appeal erred in holding plaintiff's first *Tameny* theory to have been preempted by the FEHA. Because we uphold plaintiff's *Tameny* claim under the second theory advanced at trial, we need not address this aspect of the decision of the Court of Appeal.

Walnut Creek offices. In that capacity, Ms. Bruno reported to both Gantt and Gary Desser, the manager of the Walnut Creek office, as well as Brian Cullen, a technical supervisor at regional headquarters in Scottsdale, Arizona.

Shortly after she was hired, Ms. Bruno experienced sexual harassment at the hands of Desser. As the harassment continued, she complained to Gantt. He recommended she report it to Cullen in Scottsdale. Ultimately, Gantt himself contacted both Bonnie Caroline, who was responsible for receiving complaints of sexual discrimination, and Dave Berg, his immediate supervisor, about the problem. Despite these reports, the harassment continued. Accordingly, Gantt took it upon himself to speak a second time with both Berg and Ms. Caroline. Finally, in early 1981, Desser was demoted from sales manager to sales representative and replaced by Robert Warren. In March, Ms. Bruno was transferred to a sales representative position. A month later, however, she was fired.

Gantt stated that he was present at the April meeting in which Berg directed Warren to fire Bruno and ridiculed Gantt for supporting her. The following month, Berg himself resigned from Sentry following an investigation into claims that he had engaged in sexual harassment. Berg's replacement, Frank Singer, assumed the title "Director of Sales" and recruited John Tailby to assume Berg's old position supervising the various sales offices. According to one witness, Tailby said Singer told him that getting rid of Gantt was to be one of his first tasks. Tailby resisted, however, and in 1981 Gantt was ranked among Sentry's top district managers in premium growth.

Bruno, meanwhile, filed a complaint with the Department of Fair Employment and Housing (DFEH). She alleged harassment by Desser and failure by Sentry's higher management to act on her complaints. Caroline Fribance, Sentry's house counsel in charge of labor-related matters, undertook to investigate the matter. Gantt informed Fribance that he had reported Bruno's complaints to personnel in Scottsdale. However, Gantt gained the impression that he was being pressured by Fribance to retract his claim that he had informed Scottsdale of the complaints. Later, following the interview with Fribance, Tailby cautioned Gantt that Singer and others in the company did not care for Gantt. In a follow-up memorandum, Tailby cautioned Gantt that "it sometimes appears that you are involved in some kind of 'intrigue' and 'undercover' operation." In December 1982, Tailby rated Gantt's overall work performance for the year as "acceptable." Without directly informing Gantt, Singer changed the rating to "borderline acceptable/unacceptable."

Shortly thereafter, John Thompson, a DFEH investigator, contacted Fribance to arrange interviews with certain employees, including Gantt. Because of his growing unease about Fribance, Gantt arranged to meet secretly with Thompson before the scheduled interview. Gantt told him the facts of which he was aware, including his reporting of Bruno's complaints to Scottsdale, and Thompson assured him that he would be protected under the law from any retaliation for his statements. Thompson gained the impression that Gantt felt he was being pressured and was extremely fearful of retaliation because of his unfavorable testimony.

* * *

Less than two months later, on March 3, 1983, Gantt attended an awards ceremony in Scottsdale to accept a life insurance sales award on behalf of his office. The following morning, Singer and Tailby informed him that he was being demoted to sales representative. Shortly thereafter, Gantt's new supervisor, Neil Whitman, warned him that he would be fired if he attempted to undermine Whitman's authority. Gantt was also informed that he would not be given a "book" of existing accounts to start his new job; according to Gantt, such a book was necessary to survive.

During the following month, Gantt was in the office only intermittently. He experienced a variety of illnesses and took vacation time and sick leave. In mid-April he was offered and accepted a position with another company. He left Sentry's payroll in early May. Two months later, he filed the instant lawsuit alleging that "as a result of the pressure applied by the defendants ... he was forced to resign."

As noted earlier, the jury returned a special verdict in favor of Gantt, finding, inter alia, that Gantt had been constructively discharged; that Sentry lacked an "honest good faith belief the termination was warranted for legally valid business reasons"; that Gantt was discharged "in retaliation for his refusal to testify untruthfully or to withhold testimony"; that Gantt was further discharged in retaliation for his "actions or statements with respect to Joyce Bruno's sexual harassment allegations;" and that in committing these acts Sentry acted with malice, oppression or fraud.

III. DISCUSSION

A. *Sources of the Public Policy Exception*

This court first recognized a public policy exception to the at-will employment doctrine in *Tameny,* and has since reaffirmed its commitment to that principle on several occasions. Indeed, following the seminal California decision in Petermann v. International Brotherhood of Teamsters (1959) 174 Cal.App.2d 184, 344 P.2d 25, the antecedent to our holding in *Tameny,* the vast majority of states have recognized that an at-will employee possesses a tort action when he or she is discharged for performing an act that public policy would encourage, or for refusing to do something that public policy would condemn.

Yet despite its broad acceptance, the principle underlying the public policy exception is more easily stated than applied. The difficulty, of course, lies in determining where and how to draw the line between claims that genuinely involve matters of public policy, and those that concern merely ordinary disputes between employer and employee. This determination depends in large part on whether the public policy alleged is sufficiently clear to provide the basis for such a potent remedy. In *Foley* we endeavored to provide some guidelines by noting that the policy in question must involve a matter that affects society at large rather than a purely personal or proprietary interest of the plaintiff or employer; in addition, the policy must be "fundamental," "substantial" and "well established" at the time of the discharge.

We declined in *Foley* to determine whether the violation of a statute or constitutional provision is invariably a prerequisite to the conclusion that a discharge violates public policy. A review of the pertinent case law in California and elsewhere, however, reveals that few courts have recognized a public policy claim absent a statute or constitutional provision evidencing the policy in question. Indeed, as courts and commentators alike have noted, the cases in which violations of public policy are found generally fall into four categories: (1) refusing to violate a statute; (2) performing a statutory obligation; (3) exercising a statutory right or privilege; and (4) reporting an alleged violation of a statute of public importance.

To be sure, those courts which have addressed the issue appear to be divided over the question whether nonlegislative sources may ever provide the basis of a public policy claim. Pierce v. Ortho Pharmaceutical Corp. (1980) 84 N.J. 58, 417 A.2d 505 is the leading case for a broad interpretation. As the New Jersey Supreme Court explained: "The sources of public policy [which may limit the employer's right of discharge] include legislation; administrative rules, regulation, or decision; and judicial decisions. In certain instances, a professional code of ethics may contain an expression of public policy." Several other states have adopted similarly broad views of the public policy exception.

Other courts have applied a stricter definition to public policy claims. The leading case is Brockmeyer v. Dun & Bradstreet (1983) 113 Wis.2d 561, 335 N.W.2d 834. There, the Wisconsin Supreme Court, while recognizing a public policy exception to the employment at-will doctrine, nevertheless limited plaintiffs to contract damages and confined such claims to statutory or constitutional violations. "Given the vagueness of the concept of public policy," the court explained, "it is necessary that we be more precise about the contours of the public policy exception. A wrongful discharge is actionable when the termination clearly contravenes the public welfare and gravely violates paramount requirements of public interest. The public policy must be evidenced by a constitutional or statutory provision." Other courts have adopted similarly restrictive views of the contours of the public policy exception.

Turning from other jurisdictions to California law, one finds the courts similarly divided. As we recently observed in *Foley*: "Several subsequent Court of Appeal cases have limited our holding [in *Tameny*] to policies derived from statute. At least three other Court of Appeal decisions addressing the issue of where policy giving rise to an action may be found have concluded in dicta that public policy, as a basis for a wrongful discharge action, need not be policy rooted in a statute or constitutional provision.

Although we have not taken a position on this precise issue, it is true, as plaintiff notes, that this court has not previously confined itself to legislative enactments when determining the public policy of the state. We have, for example, long declined to enforce contracts inimical to law or the public interest, and long ago declared racial discrimination to be contrary to public policy under the common law duty of innkeepers and common carriers to furnish accommodations to all persons.

The analogy to illegal contracts has particular force. For at root, the public policy exception rests on the recognition that in a civilized society the rights of each person are necessarily limited by the rights of others and of the public at large; this is the delicate balance which holds such societies together. Accordingly, while an at-will employee may be terminated for no reason, or for an arbitrary or irrational reason, there can be no right to terminate for an unlawful reason or a purpose that contravenes fundamental public policy. Any other conclusion would sanction lawlessness, which courts by their very nature are bound to oppose. It is a very short and logical step, therefore, from declining to enforce contracts inimical to law or the public interest, to refusing to sanction terminations in contravention of fundamental public policy. Indeed, we expressly acknowledged the analogy in *Foley*, noting, in the context of our *Tameny* discussion: "A comparison of the manner in which contracts for illegal purposes are treated is useful."

Unfortunately, as we have also previously acknowledged, "[t]he term 'public policy' is inherently not subject to precise definition .... 'By "public" policy is intended that principle of law which holds that no citizen can lawfully do that which has a tendency to be injurious to the public or against the public good ....' " It was this rather open-ended definition on which the court relied in *Petermann*, the seminal decision articulating the public policy exception to the employment at-will doctrine.

Surveying the extensive and conflicting decisional law summarized above, several general observations are possible. First, notwithstanding the lively theoretical debate over the sources of public policy which may support a wrongful discharge claim, with few exceptions courts have, in practice, relied to some extent on statutory or constitutional expressions of public policy as a basis of the employee's claim.

Second, it is generally agreed that "public policy" as a concept is notoriously resistant to precise definition, and that courts should venture into this area, if at all, with great care and due deference to the judgment of the legislative branch, "lest they mistake their own predilections for public policy which deserves recognition at law." Indeed, one of the most frequently cited decisions favoring a broad interpretation, observed that courts "should proceed cautiously" if called upon to declare public policy absent some prior legislative expression on the subject.

These wise caveats against judicial policymaking are unnecessary if one recognizes that courts in *wrongful discharge actions* may not declare public policy without a basis in either the constitution or statutory provisions. A public policy exception carefully tethered to fundamental policies that are delineated in constitutional or statutory provisions strikes the proper balance among the interests of employers, employees and the public. The employer is bound, at a minimum, to know the fundamental public policies of the state and nation as expressed in their constitutions and statutes; so limited, the public policy exception presents no impediment to employers that operate within the bounds of law. Employees are protected against employer actions that contravene fundamental state policy. And society's interests are served through a more stable job market, in which its most important policies are safeguarded.

B. *Application of the Public Policy Exception*

Here, we are *not* being asked to declare public policy. The issue as framed by the pleadings and the parties is whether there exists a clear constitutional or legislative declaration of fundamental public policy forbidding plaintiff's discharge under the facts and circumstances presented.

Initially, the parties dispute whether the discharge of an employee in retaliation for reporting a coworker's claim of sexual harassment to higher management may rise to the level of a *Tameny* violation. Sentry argues that such reporting inures only to the benefit of the employee in question rather than to the public at large, and questions the constitutional or statutory basis of such a claim. Plaintiff responds that the same constitutional provision (Cal.Const., art. I, § 8) that prohibits sexual discrimination against employees and demands a workplace free from the pernicious influence of sexual harassment also protects the employee who courageously intervenes on behalf of a harassed colleague.

Although Sentry did not discriminate against Gantt on account of his sex within the meaning of the constitutional provision, there is nevertheless direct statutory support for the jury's express finding that Sentry violated a fundamental public policy when it constructively discharged plaintiff "in retaliation for his refusal to testify untruthfully or to withhold testimony" in the course of the DFEH investigation. Indeed, *Petermann,* "one of the seminal California decisions in this area" presented the parallel situation of an employee who was dismissed from his position because he had refused to follow his employer's instructions to testify falsely under oath before a legislative committee. Such conduct, the court concluded, could not be condoned as a matter of "public policy and sound morality." "It would be obnoxious to the interests of the state and contrary to public policy and sound morality to allow an employer to discharge any employee ... on the ground that the employee declined to commit perjury, an act specifically enjoined by statute .... The public policy of this state as reflected in the Penal Code sections referred to above would be seriously impaired if it were to be held that one could be discharged by reason of his refusal to commit perjury."

We endorsed the principles of *Petermann* in *Tameny,* holding that an employee who alleged that he was discharged because he refused to participate in an illegal price fixing scheme may subject his employer "to liability for compensatory and punitive damages under normal tort principles." As we explained: "[A]n employer's authority over its employee does not include the right to demand that the employee commit a criminal act to further its interests, and an employer may not coerce compliance with such unlawful directions by discharging an employee who refuses to follow such an order. An employer engaging in such conduct violates a basic duty imposed by law upon all employers, and thus an employee who has suffered damages as a result of such discharge may maintain a tort action for wrongful discharge against the employer."

The instant case fits squarely within the rubric of *Petermann* and *Tameny.* The FEHA specifically enjoins any obstruction of a DFEH investigation. Government Code section 12975 provides: "Any person who shall willfully resist, prevent, impede or interfere with any member of the department or the commission or any of its agents or employees in the performance of duties pursuant to the provisions of this part relating to employment discrimination, ... is guilty of a misdemeanor" punishable by fine or imprisonment. Nowhere in our society is the need greater than in protecting well motivated employees who come forward to testify truthfully in an administrative investigation of charges of discrimination based on sexual harassment. It is self-evident that few employees would cooperate with such investigations if the price were retaliatory discharge from employment.

Thus, any attempt to induce or coerce an employee to lie to a DFEH investigator plainly contravenes the public policy of this State.

Accordingly, we hold that plaintiff established a valid *Tameny* claim based on the theory of retaliation for refusal to withhold information or to provide false information to the DFEH.

C. *The Workers' Compensation Act Does Not Preempt the Tameny Claim*

* * *

In sum, we hold that the Workers' Compensation Act does not preempt plaintiff's *Tameny* action for tortious discharge in contravention of fundamental public policy.

The judgment of the Court of Appeal is affirmed.

BALLA v. GAMBRO, INC.
145 Ill.2d 492, 164 Ill.Dec. 892, 584 N.E.2d 104 (1991).

CLARK, JUSTICE: The issue in this case is whether in-house counsel should be allowed the remedy of an action for retaliatory discharge.

Appellee, Roger Balla, formerly in-house counsel for Gambro, Inc. (Gambro), filed a retaliatory discharge action against Gambro, its affiliate Gambro Dialysatoren, KG (Gambro Germany), its parent company Gambro Lundia, AB (Gambro Sweden), and the president of Gambro in the circuit court of Cook County (Gambro, Gambro Germany and Gambro Sweden collectively referred to as appellants). Appellee alleged that he was fired in contravention of Illinois public policy and sought damages for the discharge. The trial court dismissed the action on appellants' motion for summary judgment. The appellate court reversed.

Gambro is a distributor of kidney dialysis equipment manufactured by Gambro Germany. Among the products distributed by Gambro are dialyzers which filter excess fluid and toxic substances from the blood of patients with no or impaired kidney function. The manufacture and sale of dialyzers is regulated by the United States Food and Drug Administration (FDA); the Federal Food, Drug, and Cosmetic Act (Federal Act) (21 U.S.C. § 331 et seq. (1988)); FDA regulations (21 C.F.R. §§ 820.150 through 820.198 (1987)); and the Illinois Food, Drug and Cosmetic Act (Ill.Rev.Stat.1985, ch. 56½, par. 501 et seq.).

Appellee, Roger J. Balla, is and was at all times throughout this controversy an attorney licensed to practice law in the State of Illinois. On March 17, 1980, appellee executed an employment agreement with Gambro which contained the terms of appellee's employment. Generally, the employment agreement provided that appellee would "be responsible for all legal matters within the company and for personnel within the company's sales office." Appellee held the title of director of adminsitration at Gambro. As director of administration, appellee's specific responsibilities included, inter alia: advising, counseling and representing management on legal matters: establishing and administering personnel policies; coordinating and overseeing corporate activities to assure compliance with applicable laws and regulations, and preventing or minimizing legal or administrative proceedings; and coordinating the activities of the manager of regulatory affairs. Regarding this last responsibility, under Gambro's corporate hierarchy, appellee supervised the manager of regulatory affairs, and the manager reported directly to appellee.

In August 1983, the manager of regulatory affairs for Gambro left the company and appellee assumed the manager's specific duties. Although appellee's original employment agreement was not modified to reflect his new position, his annual compensation was increased and Gambro's corporate organizational chart referred to appellee's positions as "Dir. of Admin./Personnel; General Counsel; Mgr. of Regulatory Affairs." The job description for the position described the manager as an individual "responsible for ensuring awareness of and compliance with federal, state and local laws and regulations affecting the company's operations and products." Requirements for the position were a bachelor of science degree and three to five years in the medical device field plus two years experience in the area of government regulations. The individual in the position prior to appellee was not an attorney.

In July 1985 Gambro Germany informed Gambro in a letter that certain dialyzers it had manufactured, the clearances of which varied from the package insert, were about to be shipped to Gambro. Referring to these dialyzers, Gambro Germany advised Gambro:

> "For acute patients risk is that the acute uremic situation will not be improved in spite of the treatment, giving continuous high levels of potassium, phosphate and urea/creatine. The chronic patient may note the effect as a slow progression of the uremic situation and depending on the interval between medical check-ups the medical risk may not be overlooked."

Appellee told the president of Gambro to reject the shipment because the dialyzers did not comply with FDA regulations. The president notified Gambro Germany of its decision to reject the shipment on July 12, 1985.

However, one week later the president informed Gambro Germany that Gambro would accept the dialyzers and "sell [them] to a unit that is not currently our customer but who buys only on price." Appellee contends that he was not informed by the president of the decision to accept the dialyzers but became aware of it through other Gambro employees. Appellee maintains that he spoke with the president in August regarding the company's decision to accept the dialyzers and told the president that he would do whatever necessary to stop the sale of the dialyzers.

On September 4, 1985, appellee was discharged from Gambro's employment by its president. The following day, appellee reported the shipment of the dialyzers to the FDA. The FDA seized the shipment and determined the product to be "adulterated within the meaning of section 501(h) of the [Federal Act]."

On March 19, 1986, appellee filed a four-count complaint in tort for retaliatory discharge seeking $22 million in damages. Counts III and IV for emotional distress were dismissed from the action, as was the president in an order entered by the trial court on November 5, 1986.

On July 28, 1987, Gambro filed a motion for summary judgment. Gambro argued that appellee, as an attorney, was precluded from filing a retaliatory discharge action in light of the appellate court opinion in Herbster v. North American Co. for Life & Health Insurance (1986), 150 Ill.App.3d 21. Gambro Germany and Gambro Sweden joined in Gambro's motion. Appellee argued that while the *Herbster* opinion declined to extend the tort of retaliatory discharge to the plaintiff/attorney before the court, the opinion did not foreclose the possibility of extending the tort in the future. Appellee argued that the plaintiff in *Herbster* was in-house counsel for a corporation whose duties were restricted to legal matters; whereas he served as the director of administration and personnel and manager of regulatory affairs as well as general counsel for Gambro. Appellee argued that a question of fact existed as to whether he was discharged for the performance of a purely legal function.

On November 30, 1988, the trial court granted appellants' motion for summary judgment. In its opinion, the trial court specifically stated that "the very ground [appellee is] claiming as the basis for retaliatory discharge all [sic] involves the decisions which he made applying law to fact to determine whether these things complied with the federal regulations, and that is clearly legal work." Thus, the trial court concluded that the duties appellee was performing which led to his discharge were "conduct clearly within the attorney-client relationship" and that Gambro had the "absolute right" to discharge its attorney. On appeal, the court below held that an attorney is not barred as a matter of law from bringing an action for retaliatory discharge. Rather, determination of whether an attorney has standing to bring the action was based on the following three-part test:

> "(1) whether [the attorney's] discharge resulted from information he learned as a 'layman' in a nonlegal position; (2) whether [the attorney] learned the information as a result of the attorney/client relationship, if so, whether the information was privileged, and if it was privileged, whether the privilege was waived; and (3) whether there were any countervailing public policies favoring disclosure of privileged information learned from the attorney/client relationship."

The court remanded for a determination of these questions of fact.

We agree with the trial court that appellee does not have a cause of action against Gambro for retaliatory discharge under the facts of the case at bar. Generally, this court adheres to the proposition that " 'an employer may discharge an employee-at-will for any reason or for no reason [at all].' " However, in Kelsay v. Motorola, Inc. (1978), 74 Ill.2d 172, this court first recognized the limited and narrow tort of retaliatory discharge. In *Kelsay*, an at-will employee was fired for filing a worker's compensation claim against her employer. After examining the history and purpose behind the Workers' Compensation Act to determine the public policy behind its enactment, this court held that the employee should have a cause of action for retaliatory discharge. This court stressed that if employers could fire employees for filing workers' compensation claims, the public policy behind the enactment of the Workers' Compensation Act would be frustrated.

Subsequently, in Palmateer v. International Harvester Co. (1981), 85 Ill.2d 124, this court again examined the tort of retaliatory discharge. In *Palmateer*, an employee was discharged for informing the police of suspected criminal activities of a co-employee, and because he agreed to provide assistance in any investigation and trial of the matter. Based on the public policy favoring the investigation and prosecution of crime, this court held that the employee had a cause of action for retaliatory discharge. Further, we stated:

> "All that is required [to bring a cause of action for retaliatory discharge] is that the employer discharge the employee in retaliation for the employee's activities, and that the discharge be in contravention of a clearly mandated public policy."

In this case it appears that Gambro discharged appellee, an employee of Gambro, in retaliation for his activities, and this discharge was in contravention of a clearly mandated public policy. Appellee allegedly told the president of Gambro that he would do whatever was necessary to stop the sale of the "misbranded and/or adulterated" dialyzers. In appellee's eyes, the use of these dialyzers could cause death or serious bodily harm to patients. As we have stated before, "[t]here is no public policy more important or more fundamental than the one favoring the effective protection of the lives and property of citizens." However, in this case, appellee was not just an employee of Gambro, but also general counsel for Gambro.

As noted earlier, in Herbster v. North American Co. for Life & Health Insurance (1986), 150 Ill.App.3d 21, our appellate court held that the plaintiff, an employee and chief legal counsel for the defendant company, did not have a claim for retaliatory discharge against the company due to the presence of the attorney-client relationship. Under the facts of that case, the defendant company allegedly requested the plaintiff to destroy or remove discovery information which had been requested in lawsuits pending against the company. The plaintiff refused arguing that such conduct would constitute fraud and violate several provisions of the Illinois Code of Professional Responsibility. Subsequently, the defendant company discharged the plaintiff.

The appellate court refused to extend the tort of retaliatory discharge to the plaintiff in *Herbster* primarily because of the special relationship between an attorney and client. The court stated:

> "The mutual trust, exchanges of confidence, reliance on judgment, and personal nature of the attorney-client relationship demonstrate the unique position attorneys occupy in our society."

The appellate court recited a list of factors which make the attorney-client relationship special such as: the attorney-client privilege regarding confidential communications, the fiduciary duty an attorney owes to a client, the right of the client to terminate the relationship with or without cause, and the fact that a client has exclusive control over the subject matter of the litigation and a client may dismiss or settle a cause of action regardless of the attorney's advice. Thus, in *Herbster*, since the plaintiff's duties pertained strictly to legal matters, the appellate court determined that the plaintiff did not have a claim for retaliatory discharge.

We agree with the conclusion reached in *Herbster* that, generally, in-house counsel do not have a claim under the tort of retaliatory discharge. However, we base our decision as much on the nature and purpose of the tort of retaliatory discharge, as on the effect on the attorney-client relationship that extending the tort would have. In addition, at this time, we caution that our holding is confined by the fact that appellee is and was at all times throughout this controversy an attorney licensed to practice law in the State of Illinois. Appellee is and was subject to the Illinois Code of Professional Responsibility adopted by this court. The tort of retaliatory discharge is a limited and narrow exception to the general rule of at-will employment. The tort seeks to achieve " 'a proper balance * * * among the employer's interest in operating a business efficiently and profitably, the employee's interest in earning a livelihood, and society's interest in seeing its public policies carried out.' " Further, as stated in *Palmateer*, *"[t]he foundation of the tort of retaliatory discharge lies in the protection of public policy * * *."*

In this case, the public policy to be protected, that of protecting the lives and property of citizens, is adequately safeguarded without extending the tort of retaliatory discharge to in-house counsel. Appellee was required under the Rules of Professional Conduct to report Gambro's intention to sell the "misbranded and/or adulterated" dialyzers. Rule 1.6(b) of the Rules of Professional Conduct reads:

"A lawyer *shall* reveal information about a client to the extent it appears necessary to prevent the client from committing an act that would result in death or serious bodily injury."

Appellee alleges, and the FDA's seizure of the dialyzers indicates, that the use of the dialyzers would cause death or serious bodily injury. Thus, under the above-cited rule, appellee was under the mandate of this court to report the sale of these dialyzers.

In his brief to this court, appellee argues that not extending the tort of retaliatory discharge to in-house counsel would present attorneys with a "Hobson's choice." According to appellee, in-house counsel would face two alternatives: either comply with the client/employer's wishes and risk both the loss of a professional license and exposure to criminal sanctions, or decline to comply with client/employer's wishes and risk the loss of a full-time job and the attendant benefits. We disagree. Unlike the employees in *Kelsay* which this court recognized would be left with the difficult decision of choosing between whether to file a workers' compensation claim and risk being fired, or retaining their jobs and losing their right to a remedy, in-house counsel plainly are not confronted with such a dilemma. In-house counsel do not have a choice of whether to follow their ethical obligations as attorneys licensed to practice law, or follow the illegal and unethical demands of their clients. In-house counsel must abide by the Rules of Professional Conduct. Appellee had no choice but to report to the FDA Gambro's intention to sell or distribute these dialyzers, and consequently protect the aforementioned public policy.

In addition, we believe that extending the tort of retaliatory discharge to in-house counsel would have an undesirable effect on the attorney-client relationship that exists between these employers and their in-house counsel. Generally, a client may discharge his attorney at any time, with or without cause. This rule applies equally to in-house counsel as it does to outside counsel. Further, this rule "recognizes that the relationship between an attorney and client is based on trust and that the client must have confidence in his attorney in order to ensure that the relationship will function properly." As stated in *Herbster,* "the attorney is placed in the unique position of maintaining a close relationship with a client where the attorney receives secrets, disclosures, and information that otherwise would not be divulged to intimate friends. We believe that if in-house counsel are granted the right to sue their employers for retaliatory discharge, employers might be less willing to be forthright and candid with their in-house counsel. Employers might be hesitant to turn to their in-house counsel for advice regarding potentially questionable corporate conduct knowing that their in-house counsel could use this information in a retaliatory discharge suit.

* * *

For the foregoing reasons, the decision of the appellate court is reversed, and the decision of the trial court is affirmed.

Appellate court reversed; circuit court affirmed.

FREEMAN, JUSTICE, dissenting: I respectfully dissent from the decision of my colleagues. In concluding that the plaintiff attorney, serving as corporate in-house counsel, should not be allowed a claim for retaliatory discharge, the majority first reasons that the public policy implicated in this case, *i.e.,* protecting the lives and property of Illinois citizens, is adequately safeguarded by the lawyer's ethical obligation to reveal information about a client as necessary to prevent acts that would result in death or serious bodily harm. I find this reasoning fatally flawed.

The majority so reasons because, as a matter of law, an attorney cannot even contemplate ignoring his ethical obligations in favor of continuing in his employment. I agree with this conclusion "as a matter of law." However, to say that the categorical nature of ethical obligations is sufficient to ensure that the ethical obligations will be satisfied simply ignores reality. Specifically, it ignores that, as unfortunate for society as it may be, attorneys are no less human than nonattorneys and, thus, no less given to the temptation to either ignore or rationalize away their ethical obligations when complying therewith may render them unable to feed and support their families.

I would like to believe, as my colleagues apparently conclude, that attorneys will always "do the right thing" because the law says that they must. However, my knowledge of human nature, which is not much greater than the average layman's, and, sadly, the recent scandals involving the bench and bar of Illinois are more than sufficient to dispel such a belief. Just as the ethical obligations of the lawyers and judges involved in those scandals were inadequate to ensure that they would not break the law, I am afraid that the lawyer's ethical obligation to "blow the whistle" is likewise an inadequate safeguard for the public policy of protecting lives and property of Illinois citizens.

As reluctant as I am to concede it, the fact is that this court must take whatever steps it can, within the bounds of the law, to give lawyers incentives to abide by their ethical obligations, beyond the satisfaction inherent in their doing so. We cannot continue to delude ourselves and the people of the State of Illinois that attorneys' ethical duties, alone, are always sufficient to guarantee that lawyers will "do the right thing." In the context of this case, where doing "the right thing" will often result in termination by an employer bent on doing the "wrong thing," I believe that the incentive needed is recognition of a cause of action for retaliatory discharge, in the appropriate case.

The majority also bases its holding upon the reasoning that allowing in-house counsel a cause of action for retaliatory discharge will have a chilling effect on the attorney-client relationship and the free flow of information necessary to that relationship. This reasoning completely ignores what is very often one of the basic purposes of the attorney-client relationship, especially in the corporate client-in-house counsel setting. More importantly, it gives preeminence to the public policy favoring an unfettered right to discharge an attorney, although "[t]here is no public policy more important or more fundamental than the one favoring the effective protection of the lives and property of citizens."

* * *

Preliminarily, I would note that were an employee's desire to obey and follow the law an insufficient basis for a retaliatory discharge claim, *Palmateer* would have been decided differently. In this regard, I do not believe any useful purpose is served by distinguishing attorneys from ordinary citizens. It is incontrovertible that the law binds all men, kings and paupers alike. An attorney should not be punished simply because he has ethical obligations imposed upon him over and above the general obligation to obey the law which all men have. Nor should a corporate employer be protected simply because the employee it has discharged for "blowing the whistle" happens to be an attorney.

Notes and Questions

1. For a similar result, see Nordling v. Northern State Power Co., 478 N.W.2d 498 (Minn.1991) (attorney-client privilege bars wrongful discharge action by in-house counsel who was discharged for objecting to outside attorney's recommendation to investigate personal lifestyle of employees through surveillance).

2. What would be the effect of applying the majority's "ethics" argument to other professionals, such as physicians?

3. For a further discussion, see Giesel, The Ethics or Employment Dilemma of In–House Counsel, 5 Geo.J.Legal Ethics 535 (1992); Note, In–House Counsel's Right to Sue for Retaliatory Discharge, 92 Colum.L.Rev. ___ (1992); Note, Balla v. Gambro: Retaliatory Discharge of In–House Counsel, 5 Geo.J.Legal Ethics 633 (1992).

Page 855. Please add the following to note 2.

In Harrison v. Edison Brothers Apparel Stores, Inc., 924 F.2d 530 (4th Cir.1991), an employee was discharged after she refused to have sexual intercourse with her employer. The Fourth Circuit held that under North Carolina law, exchanging sexual intercourse for the economic benefit of continued employment constituted prostitution; therefore, the plaintiff was fired for refusing to perform an illegal act, in violation of the public policy exception.

Page 856. Please add the following to note 3.

See Knight v. Pillsbury Co., 761 F.Supp. 618 (S.D.Ind.1990) (no cause of action for constructive retaliatory discharge in violation of public policy).

Page 857. Please add the following to note 7.

See also Haynes v. Zoological Society, 567 N.E.2d 1048 (Ohio C.P.1990) (zoo liable for retaliatory demotion of employee who reported safety concerns to OSHA).

Page 858. Please add the following to note 8.

In Winters v. Houston Chronicle Publishing Co., 795 S.W.2d 723 (Tex. 1990), an employee was fired for reporting to management suspected illegal activities of his fellow employees, including theft, false record-keeping, and kickback schemes. The court held that there was no cause of action for the reporting of illegal activities.

Page 863. Please add the following to the end of the page.

q. A truck driver was fired for refusing to drive a vehicle without proper registration papers. See DeSoto v. Yellow Freight Systems, Inc., 957 F.2d 655 (9th Cir.1992) (held: no claim for wrongful discharge).

2. BREACH OF CONTRACT

Page 867. Please add the following notes.

8. An employee who was working under a written contract brought an action for defamation against his employer. The employer believed that the defamation action was groundless and that filing the action caused him to lose the trust, confidence, and respect of his peers and superiors. He was therefore fired. Has the employer breached the written contract, which required "just cause" for termination? See Tacket v. Delco Remy, 959 F.2d 650 (7th Cir.1992) (held: yes).

9. A former law firm associate alleged that she quit her former job and accepted an offer to head up the firm's environmental law section after a partner of the firm misrepresented that the firm had recently secured a large environmental client. After she was fired from her job, she sues alleging fraud and negligent misrepresentation. What result? See Stewart v. Jackson & Nash, 778 F.Supp. 790 (S.D.N.Y.1991) (held: no exception to at will rule for fraudulent inducement; lack of fiduciary relationship at time of bargaining bars claim for negligent misrepresentation).

Page 877. Please add the following to note 12.

See Doherty v. Doherty Insurance Agency, Inc., 878 F.2d 546 (1st Cir.1989) (oral agreement to provide retirement benefits for life enforceable and not subject to statute of frauds because a contract for lifetime benefits could be performed within a year).

Page 884. Please add the following to note 1.

In Rowe v. Montgomery Ward & Co., 437 Mich. 627, 473 N.W.2d 268 (1991), the court held that oral statements of job security must be clear and unequivocal. *Toussaint* was limited to situations where an employee was engaged in preemployment negotiations about job security and the personnel manual was given to "memorialize" a promise of job security.

Page 885. Please add the following note.

4A. If an employer may unilaterally change the terms of an employment handbook, how, if at all, must these changes be communicated to the employee? See Durtsche v. American Colloid Co., 958 F.2d 1007 (10th Cir.1992) (inconspicuous changes in a handbook were ineffective to notify an employee of change in his status from permanent employee to at-will employee). Cf. Adams v. Square D. Co., 775 F.Supp. 869 (D.S.C.1991) (new handbook, issued after employee was hired and which made employment at-will, superseded implied promises in prior handbook).

Page 886. Please add the following to note 8.

Compare Swanson v. Liquid Air Corp., 118 Wash.2d 512, 826 P.2d 664 (1992) (disclaimer in handbook requires reasonable notice) and McDonald v. Mobil Coal Producing, Inc., 820 P.2d 986 (Wyo.1991) (inconspicuous disclaimer in handbook invalid) with Suter v. Harsco Corp., 184 W.Va. 734, 403 S.E.2d 751 (1991) (implied promise in handbook negated by express disclaimer on employment application).

C. OTHER COMMON LAW AND STATUTORY PROTECTIONS FROM DISCHARGE

1. COMMON LAW

Page 907. Please omit the main case and replace it with the following two cases.

WILSON v. MONARCH PAPER CO.
939 F.2d 1138 (5th Cir.1991).

E. Grady Jolly, Circuit Judge:

In this employment discrimination case, Monarch Paper Company, et al., appeals a $3,400,000 jury verdict finding it liable for age discrimination and retaliation under the Age Discrimination in Employment Act (ADEA), 29 U.S.C. § 621, and for intentional infliction of emotional distress under Texas state law. Monarch challenges the sufficiency of the evidence. It also challenges the district court's denial of their motions for directed verdict, for judgment non obstante veredicto (JNOV), for new trial, and for remittitur. Upon review of the entire record, we affirm.

Because Monarch is challenging the sufficiency of the evidence, the facts are recited in the light most favorable to the jury's verdict. In 1970, at age 48, Richard E. Wilson was hired by Monarch Paper Company. Monarch is an incorporated division of Unisource Corporation, and Unisource is an incorporated group of Alco Standard Corporation. Wilson served as manager of the Corpus Christi division until November 1, 1977, when he was moved to the corporate staff in Houston to serve as "Corporate Director of Physical Distribution." During that time, he routinely received merit raises and performance bonuses. In 1980, Wilson received the additional title of "Vice President." In 1981, Wilson was given the additional title of "Assistant to John Blankenship," Monarch's President at the time.

While he was Director of Physical Distribution, Wilson received most of his assignments from Blankenship. Blankenship always seemed pleased with Wilson's performance and Wilson was never reprimanded or counseled about his performance. Blankenship provided Wilson with objective performance criteria at the beginning of each year, and Wilson's bonuses at the end of the year were based on his good performance under that objective criteria. In 1981, Wilson was placed in charge of the completion of an office warehouse building in Dallas, the largest construction project Monarch had ever undertaken. Wilson successfully completed that project within budget.

In 1981, Wilson saw a portion of Monarch's long-range plans that indicated that Monarch was presently advancing younger persons in all levels of Monarch management. Tom Davis, who was hired as Employee Relations Manager of Monarch in 1979, testified that from the time he started to work at Monarch, he heard repeated references by the division managers (including Larry Clark, who later became the Executive Vice President of Monarch) to the age of employees on the corporate staff, including Wilson.

In October 1981, Blankenship became Chairman of Monarch and Unisource brought in a new, 42–year–old president from outside the company, Hamilton Bisbee. An announcement was made that Larry Clark would be assuming expanded responsibilities in physical distribution. According to the defendants, one of Blankenship's final acts as President was to direct Clark (who was in his mid-forties at the time) to assume expanded responsibility for both the operational and physical distribution aspects of Monarch.

When Bisbee arrived at Monarch in November 1981, Wilson was still deeply involved in the Dallas construction project. Richard Gozon, who was 43 years old and the President of Unisource, outlined Blankenship's new responsibilities as Chairman of the company and requested that Blankenship, Bisbee, Wilson, and John Hartley of Unisource "continue to work very closely together on the completion of the Dallas project." Bisbee, however, refused to speak to Wilson or to "interface" with him. This "silent treatment" was apparently tactical; Bisbee later told another Monarch employee, Bill Shehan, "if I ever stop talking to you, you're dead." Shehan also testified that at a meeting in Philadelphia at about the time Bisbee became President of Monarch, Gozon told Bisbee, "I'm not telling you that you have to fire Dick Wilson. I'm telling you that he cannot make any more money."

* * *

Blankenship was diagnosed with cancer in February 1982. In March 1982, Wilson was hospitalized for orthopedic surgery. Immediately after Blankenship's death in June 1982, Bisbee and Snelgrove gave Wilson three options: (1) he could take a sales job in Corpus Christi at half his pay; (2) he could be terminated with three months' severance pay; or (3) he could accept a job as warehouse supervisor in the Houston warehouse at the same salary but with a reduction in benefits. The benefits included participation in the management bonus plan, and the loss of the use of a company car, a company club membership, and a company expense account.

Wilson accepted the warehouse position. Wilson believed that he was being offered the position of Warehouse Manager, the only vacant position in the Houston warehouse at the time. When Wilson reported for duty at the warehouse on August 16, 1982, however, he was placed instead in the position of an entry level supervisor, a position that required no more than one year's experience in the paper business. Wilson, with his thirty years of experience in the paper business and a college degree, was vastly overqualified and overpaid for that position.

Soon after he went to the warehouse, Wilson was subjected to harassment and verbal abuse by his supervisor, Operations Manager and Acting Warehouse Manager Paul Bradley (who had previously been subordinate to Wilson). Bradley referred to Wilson as "old man" and admitted posting a sign in the warehouse that said "Wilson is old." In Bradley's absence, Wilson was placed under the supervision of a man in his twenties. Finally, Wilson was further demeaned when he was placed in charge of housekeeping but was not given any employees to assist him in the housekeeping duties. Wilson, the former vice-president and assistant to the president, was thus reduced finally to sweeping the floors and cleaning up the employees' cafeteria, duties which occupied 75 percent of his working time.

In the late fall of 1982, Wilson began suffering from respiratory problems caused by the dusty conditions in the warehouse and stress from the unrelenting harassment by his employer. On January 6, 1983, Wilson left work to see a doctor about his respiratory problems.

He was advised to stay out of a dusty environment and was later advised that he had a clinically significant allergy to dust. Shortly after January 6, 1983, Wilson consulted a psychiatrist who diagnosed him as suffering from reactive depression, possibly suicidal, because of on-the-job stress. The psychiatrist also advised that Wilson should stay away from work indefinitely.

Wilson filed an age discrimination charge with the EEOC in January 1983. Although he continued being treated by a psychiatrist, his condition deteriorated to the point that in March 1983, he was involuntarily hospitalized with a psychotic manic episode. Prior to the difficulties with his employer, Wilson had no history of emotional illness.

Wilson's emotional illness was severe and long-lasting. He was diagnosed with manic-depressive illness or bipolar disorder. After his first hospitalization for a manic episode, in which he was locked in a padded cell and heavily sedated, he fell into a deep depression. The depression was unremitting for over two years and necessitated an additional hospital stay in which he was given electroconvulsive therapy (shock treatments). It was not until 1987 that Wilson's illness began remission, thus allowing him to carry on a semblance of a normal life.

On February 27, 1984, Wilson filed suit against the defendants, alleging age discrimination and various state law tort and contract claims. The defendants filed a counterclaim, seeking damages in excess of $10,000 for libel and slander, but later dismissed it. Before trial, the district court dismissed one of Wilson's claims on the basis of factual or legal insufficiency. The court also dismissed his emotional distress claim to the extent that "the alleged conduct occurred in the administration of [defendants'] disability plan" on grounds of ERISA preemption. On November 30 and December 28, 1988, the case was tried before a jury on Wilson's remaining claims that the defendants (1) reassigned him because of his age; (2) intentionally inflicted emotional distress; and (3) terminated his long-term disability benefits in retaliation for filing charges of age discrimination under the Age Discrimination in Employment Act (ADEA).

The district court denied the defendants' motions for directed verdict. The jury returned a special verdict in favor of Wilson on his age discrimination claim, awarding him $156,000 in damages, plus an equal amount in liquidated damages. The jury also found in favor of Wilson on his claim for intentional infliction of emotional distress, awarding him past damages of $622,359.15, future damages of $225,000, and punitive damages of $2,250,000. The jury found in favor of the defendants on Wilson's retaliation claim. The district court entered judgment for $3,409,359.15 plus prejudgment interest. The district court denied the defendants' motions for judgment NOV, new trial, or, alternatively, a remittitur. The defendants appeal.

* * *

Wilson's claim for intentional infliction of emotional distress is a pendent state law claim. As such, we are bound to apply the law of Texas in determining whether the defendant's motions should have been granted. The Texas Supreme Court has not expressly recognized the tort of intentional infliction of emotional distress. We, however, have nonetheless recognized on at least two prior occasions, *see, e.g.,* Blankenship v. Kerr County, 878 F.2d 893, 898 (5th Cir.1989) and Dean v. Ford Motor Credit Co., 885 F.2d 300 (5th Cir.1989), that such a cause of action exists in Texas, based on the Texas Court of Appeals' decision in Tidelands Auto. Club v. Walters, 699 S.W.2d 939 (Tex.App.—Beaumont 1985, writ ref'd n.r.e.). To prevail on a claim for intentional infliction of emotional distress, Texas law requires that the following four elements be established:

(1) that the defendant acted intentionally or recklessly;

(2) that the conduct was 'extreme and outrageous';

(3) that the actions of the defendant caused the plaintiff emotional distress; and

(4) that the emotional distress suffered by the plaintiff was severe.

The sole issue before us is whether Monarch's conduct was "extreme and outrageous."

(1)

"Extreme and outrageous conduct" is an amorphous phrase that escapes precise definition. In *Dean* however, we stated that

[l]iability [for outrageous conduct] has been found only where the conduct has been so outrageous in character, and so extreme in degree, as to go beyond all possible bounds of decency, and to be regarded as atrocious, and utterly intolerable in a civilized community .... Generally, the case is one in which a recitation of the facts to an average member of the community would lead him to exclaim, "Outrageous."

885 F.2d at 306 (citing Restatement (Second) of Torts § 46, Comment d (1965)). The Restatement also provides for some limits on jury verdicts by stating that liability "does not extend to mere insults, indignities, threats, annoyances, petty oppressions, or other trivialities .... There is no occasion for the law to intervene in every case where someone's feelings are hurt."

The facts of a given claim of outrageous conduct must be analyzed in context, and ours is the employment setting. We are cognizant that "the work culture in some situations may contemplate a degree of teasing and taunting that in other circumstances might be considered cruel and outrageous." We further recognize that properly to manage its business, every employer must on occasion review, criticize, demote, transfer, and discipline employees. We also acknowledge that it is not unusual for an employer, instead of directly discharging an employee, to create unpleasant and onerous work conditions designed to force an employee to quit, i.e., "constructively" to discharge the employee. In short, although this sort of conduct often rises to the level of illegality, except in the *most* unusual cases it is not the sort of conduct, as deplorable as it may sometimes be, that constitutes "extreme and outrageous" conduct.

(2)

Our recent decision in *Dean* is instructive in determining what types of conduct in the employment setting will constitute sufficiently outrageous conduct so as to legally support a jury's verdict. In *Dean,* the plaintiff presented evidence that (1) when she expressed interest in transferring to a higher paying position in the collection department, she was told that "women don't usually go into that department"; (2) she was denied a transfer to the collection department, and a lesser qualified man was selected; (3) the defendant's attitude toward the plaintiff changed after she complained about alleged discriminatory treatment; (4) management began to transfer her from desk to desk within the administrative department; (5) a coworker testified she believed management was trying to "set ... [the plaintiff] up"; (6) she was called upon to do more work than the other clerks "and subjected to unfair harassment"; and (7) management used "special" annual reviews (that only the plaintiff received) to downgrade her performance. Far more significant to the claim for intentional infliction of emotional distress, however, (8) the plaintiff proved that a supervisor, who had access to the employer's checks, intentionally placed checks in the plaintiff's purse in order to make it appear that she was a thief, or to put her in fear of criminal charges for theft. We expressly held that the "check incidents" were "precisely what [took] this case beyond the realm of an ordinary employment dispute and into the realm of an outrageous one." We concluded that without the "check incidents" the employer's conduct "would not have been outrageous."

Wilson argues that Monarch's conduct is sufficiently outrageous to meet the *Dean* standard; in the alternative, he argues that Monarch's actions are certainly more outrageous than the conduct in Bushell v. Dean, 781 S.W.2d 652 (Tex.App.—Austin 1989), writ denied in part, rev'd in part on other grounds, 803 S.W.2d 711 (Tex.1991), which is a recent pronouncement by the Texas courts on the subject. Monarch contends that Wilson's evidence of outrageous conduct, that is, his reassignment to a job he did not like, his strained relationship with the company president, and isolated references to his age, is the same evidence that he used to prove his age discrimination claim. According to Monarch, unless all federal court discrimination lawsuits are to be accompanied by pendent state law claims for emotional distress, this court must make it clear that ordinary employment disputes cannot support an emotional distress claim. We agree with Monarch that more is required to prove intentional infliction of emotional distress than the usual ADEA claim.

(3)

In *Dean*, we found that the "check incidents" took the case beyond an ordinary discrimination case and supported the claim of infliction of emotional distress. Wilson contends that Monarch's conduct was equally outrageous as the "check incidents" in *Dean*. Generally, Wilson argues that an average member of the community would exclaim "Outrageous!" upon hearing that a 60–year–old man, with 30 years of experience in his industry, was subjected to a year-long campaign of harassment and abuse because his company wanted to force him out of his job as part of its expressed written goal of getting rid of older employees and moving younger people into management. More precisely, Wilson argues that substantial evidence of outrageous conduct supports the jury's verdict, including: (1) his duties in physical distribution were assigned to a younger person; (2) Bisbee deliberately refused to speak to him in the hallways of Monarch in order to harass him; (3) certain portions of Monarch's long-range plans expressed a desire to move younger persons into sales and management positions; (4) Bisbee wanted to replace Wilson with a younger person; (5) other managers within Monarch would not work with Wilson, and he did not receive his work directly from Bisbee; (6) he was not offered a fully guaranteed salary to transfer to Corpus Christi; (7) he was assigned to Monarch's Houston warehouse as a supervisor, which was "demeaning"; (8) Paul Bradley, the Warehouse Manager, and other Monarch managers, referred to Wilson as old; (9) Bradley prepared a sign stating "Wilson is old" and, subsequently, "Wilson is a Goldbrick"; and (10) Monarch filed a counterclaim against Wilson in this action. We are not in full agreement.

Most of Monarch's conduct is similar in degree to conduct in *Dean* that failed to reach the level of outrageousness. We hold that all of this conduct, except as explicated below, is within the "realm of an ordinary employment dispute," and, in the context of the employment milieu, is not so extreme and outrageous as to be properly addressed outside of Wilson's ADEA claim.

(4)

Wilson argues, however, that what takes this case out of the realm of an ordinary employment dispute is the degrading and humiliating way that he was stripped of his duties and demoted from an executive manager to an entry level warehouse supervisor with menial and demeaning duties. We agree. Wilson, a college graduate with thirty years experience in the paper field, had been a long-time executive at Monarch. His title was Corporate Director of Physical Distribution, with the added title of Vice–President and Assistant to the President. He had been responsible for the largest project in the company's history, and had completed the project on time and under budget. Yet, when transferred to the warehouse, Wilson's primary duty became housekeeping chores around the warehouse's shipping and receiving area. Because Monarch did not give Wilson any employees to supervise or assist him, Wilson was frequently required to sweep the warehouse. In addition, Wilson also was reduced to cleaning up after the employees in the warehouse cafeteria after their lunch hour. Wilson spent 75 percent of his time performing these menial, janitorial duties.

Monarch argues that assigning an executive with a college education and thirty years experience to janitorial duties is not extreme and outrageous conduct. The jury did not agree and neither do we. We find it difficult to conceive a workplace scenario more painful and embarrassing than an executive, indeed a vice-president and the assistant to the president, being subjected before his fellow employees to the most menial janitorial services and duties of cleaning up after entry level employees: the steep downhill push to total humiliation was complete. The evidence, considered as a whole, will fully support the view, which the jury apparently held, that Monarch, unwilling to fire Wilson outright, *intentionally and systematically* set out to humiliate him in the hopes that he would quit.[5] A reasonable jury could have found that this employer conduct was intentional and mean spirited, so severe that it resulted in institutional confinement and treatment for someone with no history of mental problems. Finally, the evidence supports the conclusion that this conduct was, indeed, so outrageous that civilized society should not tolerate it. *Dean*, 885 F.2d at 307.[6] Accordingly, the judgment of the district court in denying Monarch's

5. Nevertheless, we are not unaware of the irony in this case: if Monarch had chosen only to fire Wilson outright, leaving him without a salary, a job, insurance, etc., it would not be liable for intentional infliction of emotional distress. There is some suggestion in the record, however, that Monarch was unwilling to fire Wilson outright because it had no grounds and perhaps feared a lawsuit. Although Monarch was willing to accept Wilson's resignation, Wilson was unwilling to resign. Once he was unwilling to resign, the evidence supports the inference that Monarch's efforts intensified to force his resignation.

6. We suppose that the threat of an emotional distress claim also provides the irony of "civilizing" discrimination; or stated differently, employers will have to behave like ladies and gentlemen when discriminating.

motions for directed verdict, JNOV and a new trial on this claim is affirmed.

* * *

In conclusion, we express real concern about the consequences of applying the cause of action of intentional infliction of emotional distress to the workplace. This concern is, however, primarily a concern for the State of Texas, its courts and its legislature. Although the award in this case is astonishingly high, neither the quantum of damages, nor the applicability of punitive damages has been appealed.

For the reasons set forth above, the district court's denial of the motions for direct verdict, new trial and JNOV with respect to the intentional infliction of emotional distress verdict is AFFIRMED. The denial of Monarch's motions with respect to the age discrimination and back pay is also AFFIRMED.

Notes and Questions

1. Wilson was an at-will employee. Therefore, it would have been lawful for Monarch to tell him he was not needed in his former capacity and that the only available job was a menial job in the warehouse. What was it in the case, beyond this, that results in liability?

2. To what extent was the finding of liability affected by the magnitude of the psychological harm suffered by the plaintiff? Who should have the burden of proving that Wilson would not have had the same health problems if he were simply discharged?

3. Do you think that an appellate court with a majority of middle-aged, well-educated, and successful men was particularly sympathetic to the plight of the plaintiff?

4. In footnotes 5 and 6, the court points out the "irony" that the holding in *Wilson* could lead to more "civilized" firings of employees. Is this ironical or the essence of the case?

DIAMOND SHAMROCK REFINING & MARKETING CO. v. MENDEZ
809 S.W.2d 514 (Tex.App.1991), writ granted (Tex.1991).

CARR, JUSTICE.

Roque Mendez was terminated from his job with Diamond Shamrock Refining and Marketing Company for allegedly stealing a handful of nails. He sued Diamond Shamrock and went to the jury on two theories: that Diamond Shamrock had invaded his privacy by placing him before the public in a false light, and that Diamond Shamrock's extreme and outrageous conduct intentionally or recklessly caused him severe emotional distress. Based on favorable jury findings, Mendez was awarded a judgment from which Diamond Shamrock brings this appeal.

The Diamond Shamrock refinery at which Mendez had worked for over ten years is located in Three Rivers, a town of about 2500 people. Diamond Shamrock is the largest employer there. At the time of his discharge, Mendez was one of four chief operators at the plant.

The events culminating in his discharge occurred just before the end of the night shift on September 4, 1985. Mendez was ordered by his supervisor to clean up debris which had been left in his work area for over two weeks by maintenance personnel. This debris included loose nails discarded by carpenters working at the site. Mendez complied with the clean up order he had been given, but he was upset at what he perceived as rudeness on the part of his supervisor and the arbitrariness of the requirement that he pick up after other employees. He gathered up several loose nails, threw them in a small box, threw the box in his lunch bag, and set the bag on a shelf in the control room. He finished cleaning up the area and then went to the clock house to punch out for the day. The clock house is located on refinery property. He left work, leaving the lunch bag containing the nails on the table in the clock house where they were found by a company security guard later that morning. The nails were worth no more than $5.00.

Once at home, Mendez received a phone call from Wayne Billings, the personnel manager at the refinery. Billings asked him to return to the refinery. Upon his return, Mendez met with Billings and John Hoffman, the plant manager. Billings asked Mendez to identify the lunch bag, and Mendez indicated it was his. They asked him to explain. Mendez told them of the call he had received from the supervisor and explained that it had made him angry. He told Billings and Hoffman how he had put the nails in his lunch bag. He said he should have thrown the nails away because that is what he and the other employees had done with the other things they had had to clean up. Mendez testified that he told Billings and Hoffman that he did not intend to steal the nails. Following this explanation, Hoffman stood up and said it looked to him as if Mendez was stealing company property, and he asked if Mendez agreed. Mendez said he guessed so. Hoffman immediately terminated him and left the room. Billings asked Mendez why he had not come to him, as he could have issued Mendez a "gate pass" to take the nails off company property. Mendez replied that he did not know; he guessed he "just messed up."

There had been a series of small thefts at the refinery during the months prior to Mendez' termination, however, no one else at the refinery had been fired for stealing. The Diamond Shamrock employee handbook provided that an employee could be terminated for stealing company property.

Diamond Shamrock argues in its first point of error that there was no evidence or insufficient evidence that it had invaded Mendez' privacy by giving publicity to a matter concerning him that placed him before the public in a false light. Its first argument under this point is that it did not place Mendez in a false light; its second argument is that it did not publicize the matter.

* * *

The tort of "false light publicity" is recognized in Texas. Its elements are delineated in RESTATEMENT (SECOND) OF TORTS § 652E (1977):

> One who gives publicity to a matter concerning another that places the other before the public in a false light is subject to liability to the other for invasion of his privacy, if
>
> (a) the false light in which the other was placed would be highly offensive to a reasonable person, and
>
> (b) the actor had knowledge of or acted in reckless disregard as to the falsity of the publicized matter and the false light in which the other would be placed.

Diamond Shamrock contends that Mendez was stealing company property. Consequently, it argues that any statement that he was discharged for stealing, being true, could not have placed him in a false light. As evidence, Diamond Shamrock relies on the fact that Mendez agreed when it was suggested to him by Hoffman that he was stealing.

To prevail in a false light claim, statements must have been published about the plaintiff that are false or are at least capable of conveying a false impression about the plaintiff.

The jury was instructed that theft occurs when a person, "without the owner's consent, appropriates property with the intent to deprive the owner of said property." Mendez testified that he did not intend to steal the nails and that he did not tell anyone that he intended to steal them. When asked why he agreed with Hoffman's assessment that he was stealing, Mendez indicated that he was intimidated by the supervisors. He testified that the supervisors were always telling the employees "how everything was. And it got to a point to where you either agreed with them or, if you didn't, you were going to get fired anyway." He also testified that when he made the admission, he was unaware of the true definition of stealing. Billings testified that Mendez said he intended to steal the nails. Hoffman did not remember Mendez saying that, but he said that it was his impression from the whole conversation that Mendez intended to steal the nails.

Viewing only the evidence and inferences in favor of the jury finding, we conclude that there was evidence of probative force in support of the finding. Viewing all the evidence, we cannot say that the evidence in support of the jury's finding is so weak as to render the finding clearly wrong and manifestly unjust. Moreover, we may not substitute our judgment for that of the jury. The jury was entitled to believe Mendez' testimony.

Diamond Shamrock's second argument under its first point is that the evidence is legally and factually insufficient to support the jury's finding that it publicized the accusation of theft. Section 652E of the Restatement does not define "publicity." Comment a of section 652E refers instead to the definition at section 652D: [2]

> "Publicity," . . . means that the matter is made public, by communicating it to the public at large, or to so many persons that the matter must be regarded as substantially certain to become one of public knowledge.

RESTATEMENT (SECOND) OF TORTS § 652D comment a (1977). Widespread publicity is required.

Knowledge of Mendez' termination became disseminated throughout the Three Rivers community. Diamond Shamrock contends that there was no evidence that it was responsible for publicizing the information to the public at large. Billings, however, told his supervisors of Mendez' termination. These were people who had to know in order that Mendez' position would be filled and his duties discharged. Billings testified that the supervisors would have had to tell some of their employees, such as the operators. Clayson Royal, a chief operator, testified that Billings told him of Mendez' termination later that morning. He further testified that Billings did not use the word "steal" and that he could not remember exactly the words used, but he was under the clear impression that Mendez was terminated for stealing. Royal testified that the story of the nails in Mendez' lunch bag in the clock house was "all over the plant."

Mendez left the plant immediately after being fired without talking to anyone. He went to his parents' home and told his sister and his father that he had been fired. He told his wife that night when she came home from work. During the weeks following his termination, Mendez spoke to 100 to 125 employees about being fired. Some of them already knew he had been fired for stealing and some did not. His wife also testified that some people in Three Rivers and in nearby George West knew Mendez had been terminated for stealing, and that she told some herself. She spoke to 50 or 75 people. Neither Mendez nor his wife could name a person from the refinery who had said that he had

---

2. The Restatement actually refers to section 652C, comment a, which speaks only of an individual's proprietary interest in the exclusive use of his name or likeness. This typographical error was corrected in RESTATEMENT (SECOND) OF TORTS, Appendix §§ 588 to 707A (1989) at 362.

been terminated for stealing, although his wife added that she knew few people at the refinery.

The facts that Mendez left the plant without talking to anyone immediately after being fired, and that the story of the nails in his lunch bag was all over the plant later that morning, support the jury's conclusion that the refinery management publicized the matter "to so many persons that the matter must be regarded as substantially certain to become one of public knowledge." There was no one else who could have disseminated the story so rapidly. In fact, there was no one else who knew the story. Mendez had left the plant without talking to anyone and had gone to his parents' home where he told only his father and his sister. His sister testified that she spoke to no one other than her family about it; his father, however, was not called as a witness. Once the matter was publicized to the refinery's employees, it was not unreasonable to expect it to become common knowledge within the small community of Three Rivers. Hoffman admitted he was not surprised the reason Mendez was fired got out into the Three Rivers community. While there was evidence that Mendez and his wife told some people in the community the reason he was terminated, there were also people who approached them who already knew the story. We conclude that the evidence was sufficient to support the jury's finding.

Diamond Shamrock argues that if it did publicize the termination, it was only publicized to employees having a common interest in the publicized matter, thus giving rise to a qualified privilege excusing the publication and requiring plaintiff to prove actual malice to overcome the privilege. Diamond Shamrock's argument must fail because it did not plead the qualified privilege. It went to trial on its first amended original answer. It raised qualified privilege as an affirmative defense, but only to Mendez' libel and slander causes of action. Qualified privilege was not raised as an affirmative defense to the false light theory. The defense as to the false light theory is thus waived. Further, Diamond Shamrock failed to request a jury question regarding this affirmative defense. A defendant is required to obtain jury findings on every essential element of its affirmative defense, or the defense is waived. Diamond Shamrock's first point of error is overruled.

In its second point of error, Diamond Shamrock argues that the court erred in failing to submit a jury question inquiring whether it had knowledge of or acted in reckless disregard as to the falsity of the publicized matter and the false light in which Mendez would be placed. It argues in its third point that even if the question had been submitted, there was no evidence or insufficient evidence that Diamond Shamrock had knowledge or acted in reckless disregard. Mendez argues that Diamond Shamrock failed to preserve the error of which it complains.

The jury question presenting the false light theory reads:

Did the Defendant, Diamond Shamrock, by and through its employees, invade the privacy of the Plaintiff, Roque Mendez?

You are instructed that the Defendant may invade the privacy of the Plaintiff if it publicized matters which placed him in a false light before the public that would be highly offensive to a reasonable person.

Answer "Yes" or "No."

ANSWER: <u>Yes</u>

The standard of care set out in clause (b) of Restatement section 652E is the "actual malice" standard first enunciated in New York Times Co. v. Sullivan, 376 U.S. 254 (1964), a defamation case. Under this standard, there can be no recovery without a showing that the defendant has publicized the matter in question with knowledge that the matter is false, or with reckless disregard of whether it is false. The Court later applied this standard to a false light privacy action in Time, Inc. v. Hill, 385 U.S. 374 (1967). *Hill* involved a statutory privacy action brought by a private individual who was involved in a matter of public interest. The Court noted that the question of whether the same standard should be applicable both to persons voluntarily and involuntarily thrust into the public limelight was not before it.

The law of defamation was substantially revised in Gertz v. Robert Welch, Inc., 418 U.S. 323 (1974). That opinion left unaltered the showing of actual malice required for public officials and public figures to recover for defamation. Respecting private plaintiffs, however, the Court held that the individual states may define for themselves the appropriate standard of liability, so long as they do not impose liability without fault. In *Gertz,* the plaintiff was neither a public official nor a public figure. Therefore, his inability to prove actual malice did not impair his cause of action. He was required to prove only fault and actual injury.

Some six months after the *Gertz* decision, the Supreme Court decided Cantrell v. Forest City Pub. Co., 419 U.S. 245 (1974), a false light case. *Cantrell* involved a magazine article concerning plaintiffs who were private individuals. The trial court had instructed the jury that liability could be imposed only if it found that the false statements in the magazine article had been made with knowledge of their falsity or in reckless disregard of the truth. No objection was made to this instruction by any of the parties. Consequently, the Court noted that *Cantrell* presented no occasion to consider whether a state could constitutionally apply a more relaxed standard for a publisher of false statements injurious to a private individual under the false light theory of invasion of privacy.

The Restatement recognizes this lack of a clear standard with a caveat. RESTATEMENT (SECOND) OF TORTS § 652E caveat and comment d (1977). Comment d notes that in light of Gertz v. Robert Welch, Inc., 418 U.S. 323 (1974), it is possible that liability may be based on a showing of negligence as to truth or falsity, rather than the stricter "knowledge/reckless disregard" standard set out in clause (b) of section 652E. This leaves open the possibility that the knowledge/reckless disregard standard would apply in false light cases when the plaintiff is a public official or a public figure, and the negligence standard will apply to other plaintiffs.

Our supreme court has adopted the negligence standard for defamation cases. In Foster v. Laredo Newspapers, Inc., 541 S.W.2d 809, 819 (Tex.1976), cert. denied, 429 U.S. 1123 (1977), it held that:

> a private individual may recover damages from a publisher or broadcaster of a defamatory falsehood as compensation for actual injury upon a showing that the publisher or broadcaster knew or should have known that the defamatory statement was false.

The standard of care in Texas false light cases has not yet been resolved by our state courts. However, the Fifth Circuit Court of Appeals has considered this question in Wood v. Hustler Magazine, Inc., 736 F.2d 1084 (5th Cir.1984), cert. denied, 469 U.S. 1107 (1985), and in Braun v. Flynt, 726 F.2d 245 (5th Cir.), cert. denied sub nom., Chic Magazine, Inc. v. Braun, 469 U.S. 883 (1984). In *Braun* it was held that a publisher was not entitled to the protection of the actual malice standard in a suit by a private individual. In *Wood* the court concluded that a Texas court would apply no different standard of care to a false light claim than it would to a defamation action. It held that *Gertz* applies equally to false light and defamation cases and that Texas courts would impose liability for actual damages on publishers who negligently place private figures in an offensive false light. We agree with the *Wood* court's assessment and hold that in false light cases involving private plaintiffs the standard enunciated in *Foster* will apply. There is no question that Mendez is a private individual. Therefore, the negligence standard of care should have been included in the instruction accompanying the first jury question. The issue we must now address is whether Diamond Shamrock has preserved this error.

Diamond Shamrock objected below to the omission of the actual malice standard from the charge. It argues that its objection properly preserved the error because the issue of whether it had knowledge that the matter was false or acted in reckless disregard of its falsity is an essential element of Mendez' cause of action.

* * *

While the objection was sufficient to preserve the type of error complained of, it did not distinctly point out the actual deficiency in the instruction. It was not error to omit the actual malice instruction, but it *was* error to omit the negligence standard from the instruction. Because this is not the error Diamond Shamrock complained of in its objection, it has not preserved the error.

* * *

The judgment of the trial court is affirmed.

Notes and Questions

1. Does Mendez have a cause of action for wrongful discharge? Cf. Sabatowski v. Fisher Price Toys, 763 F.Supp. 705 (W.D.N.Y.1991) (unsuccessful wrongful discharge action brought by employee who was discharged for taking two $1 toys off an assembly line and placing them in a paper bag).

2. Cases such as *Mendez, Wilson,* and *Lewis* (p. 127), in theory, involve challenges to the *method* of discharge rather than the *fact* of discharge. To what extent are these cases concerned with the underlying reasonableness of the employer's decision to fire the employee?

2. STATUTORY PROTECTION

Page 920. Please add the following to note 5.

In Bard v. Bath Iron Works Corp., 590 A.2d 152 (Me.1991), the court declined to follow *Melchi's* holding that the complainant need only be acting in good faith. Under the Maine Whistleblowers' Protection Act, the employee also must prove that a reasonable person might have believed that the employer was acting unlawfully.

Page 926. Please add the following note.

5. Would it violate a state marital status discrimination law for an employer to have a policy requiring an employee to transfer or resign after marrying another employee in the same department? See Ross v. Stouffer Hotel Co. (Hawaii) Ltd., Inc., 72 Hawaii 350, 816 P.2d 302 (1991) (held: yes).

3. OVERLAPPING AND CONFLICTING REMEDIES

Page 934. Please add the following to note 1.

See also Thompson v. Public Service Co., 800 P.2d 1299 (Colo.1990) (defamation claim based on employer's statements in disciplinary notices not preempted by § 301).

Page 934. Please add the following to note 4.

In Ingersoll–Rand Co. v. McClendon, 111 S.Ct. 478 (1990), the Supreme Court held that ERISA preempts an employee's state law wrongful discharge claim based on his employer's desire to avoid making contributions to his pension fund. Such conduct is specifically proscribed by § 510 of ERISA.

Page 935. Please add the following to note 3.

In Screen Extras Guild, Inc. v. Superior Court, 51 Cal.3d 1017, 275 Cal.Rptr. 395, 800 P.2d 873 (1990), the Supreme Court of California held that the Labor–Management Reporting and Disclosure Act (LMRDA) preempted state causes of action for wrongful discharge and related torts when brought against a union-employer by a former management or policymaking employee. The court cited to the strong federal policy favoring union democracy, which would be furthered by not interfering with the ability of elected union leaders to carry out the will of the members they represent.

Page 935. Please add the following notes.

3A. In Barnes v. Stone Container Corp., 942 F.2d 689 (9th Cir. 1991), the Ninth Circuit held that an action brought under the Montana Wrongful Discharge From Employment Act was preempted by the NLRA.

3B. If § 301 prevents unionized employees from using statutory and common law remedies to redress wrongful discharge, leaving them to their collective bargaining remedies, are they worse off than at-will employees? All at-will employees?

D. RECONSIDERING EMPLOYMENT SECURITY

1. INTRODUCTION

Page 948. Please add the following note.

7. Although organized labor now supports efforts to reform the at will rule, this was not always the case. Many union leaders were concerned that limiting an employer's ability to terminate employees at will would eliminate the most attractive feature that unions have to offer. See Hauserman & Maranto, The Union Substitution Hypothesis Revisited: Do Judicially Created Exceptions to the Termination–At–Will Doctrine Hurt Unions?, 72 Marquette L.Rev. 317 (1989).

2. ECONOMIC EFFECTS OF WRONGFUL DISCHARGE LAW

Page 951. Please delete note 3 and insert the following.

JAMES N. DERTOUZOS & LYNN A. KAROLY, LABOR–MARKET RESPONSES TO EMPLOYER LIABILITY
35–40 (Rand Inst. for Civil Justice 1992).

4. THE ECONOMIC CONSEQUENCES
OF WRONGFUL TERMINATION

* * *

THE DIRECT LEGAL COSTS OF LITIGATION

The evolution of court doctrines granting expanded protection to employees has led to a rapid escalation of legal activity. Even though virtually nonexistent before the 1980s, there are currently 20,000 wrongful-termination cases on court dockets. These suits have been highly concentrated in states that have adopted the most liberal standards. Although general information on case disposition is not readily available, a survey of cases filed in California indicates that the potential cost of these suits is quite high. For cases going to jury trial, plaintiffs were victorious almost 70 percent of the time. On average, jury awards were nearly $700,000. In addition, defense fees were escalating over the entire period. By late 1986, defense lawyer costs could exceed $250,000 in the course of a lengthy wrongful-termination trial.

Of course, these average jury awards overstate the expenses associated with the "typical" case outcome. To begin with, averages are inflated because of the existence of a few huge awards, generally involving particularly egregious (and avoidable) behavior on the part of employers. In actuality, half of all awards in California are less than $177,000. In addition, initial awards are typically reduced by post-trial adjustments. Because of subsequent settlements and rulings during the appeal process, final payments are generally less than half of the original jury awards. From a plaintiff perspective, the value of expected payments is further reduced by the cost of waiting (final payments are typically made about 6 years after the initial filing), the 40–percent contingency fee paid to their lawyers, and the uncertainty associated with a trial (about 30 percent of them receive nothing). Indeed, the majority of employees can expect a payment that, in present value dollars, is the equivalent of a half year of work.

Given the high transaction costs associated with conducting a trial, it is not surprising that the vast majority of wrongful-termination cases settle before reaching a jury. About 95 percent of all cases settle for an average of about $25,000. With legal fees of $15,000 per case, the total average cost of a settlement is $40,000. Since settlements occur more frequently, their aggregate costs are about 2.7 times the total cost of jury trials in wrongful-termination cases.[2]

---

2. Since 95 percent of all cases settle, there are 20 times as many settlements as there are jury trials. Even following post-trial reductions in jury awards, final payments and defense fees cost employers an average of $292,000 per jury trial. Thus, an average trial is nearly five times as costly.

On an annual basis, these aggregate costs summed to over $50 million for California in 1987. However, it is important to recognize that these direct legal costs are trivial on a per-worker basis. A rough computation suggests that California has about 6 million employment-at-will employees.[3] Thus, the average cost per employee is less than $10. Even if one considers the legal expenses on a per-termination basis, the costs appear to be insignificant. Involuntary terminations typically range between 6 and 12 percent of the labor force. So, the "expected" legal cost is, at the very most, $100 per termination.

THE HIDDEN ECONOMIC COSTS OF UNJUST DISMISSAL

Even using the most liberal assumptions, it does not appear that direct legal costs are important in the aggregate. In fact, these average liabilities and litigation costs are dwarfed in comparison with standard expenses incurred as a result of labor turnover. Such costs include recruiting expenses because of the search, advertising, and interview process. In addition, training costs for firm, industry, or occupation-specific human capital can be substantial. So, what accounts for the prevailing wisdom concerning the impact of unjust dismissal doctrines?

One simple hypothesis is that the public and the business community are misinformed about the true costs of wrongful termination. Certainly, the popular perception is fueled by media accounts of the largest jury awards. At the same time, the fear of potential litigation is probably encouraged internally by those likely to benefit from an increased emphasis on avoiding the legal risks. Defense counsel, personnel-management consultants and human-resource executives all have a personal stake in promoting the deployment of preventative measures.

Even if managers had access to accurate information about the true distribution of potential litigation costs, business behavior could be dramatically affected in risk-averse firms. The potential for huge negative outcomes, even if improbable, may be very important even if per-worker liabilities are trivial. Such risk aversion is likely to be more relevant for small businesses that are unable to distribute these potential risks across numerous employees. On the other hand, some insurance companies do offer protection against wrongful-termination liabilities and defense costs. If insurance is available, premiums will reflect the advantages of risk spreading and be based on expected costs that, as we have seen, are not very high.[4]

In assessing the likely consequences of the new doctrines, it is important to recognize that all the costs of unjust dismissal are not

---

3. This excludes unionized workers, civil servants, the self-employed, and other employees protected by explicit contracts.

4. In California jury trials, nearly 40 percent of all defendants had some form of insurance against wrongful-termination liabilities. See Dertouzos, Holland, and Ebener (1988). Presumably, risk-averse firms would have strong incentives to acquire such protection.

incurred by the "firm" or its stockholders. Instead, the individual decisionmakers or personnel managers bear a disproportionate share of the costs. This could be important for several reasons. First, the computations of direct expenses ignore what could be a major cost element associated with litigation, the manager's own time. At the same time, the benefits of a "correct" decision to terminate may not accrue to the decisionmaker. In addition, even if the risks of a dismissal are prudent from a firm, senior management, or stockholder perspective, a middle manager, having fewer opportunities to diversify via a "portfolio" of decisions, may be less willing to take personnel chances. Finally, the threat of litigation implies increased oversight and second-guessing of managers. Such controversies invariably include challenges to the supervisor's previous decisions and overall competence. It may well be in the interest of personnel managers to avoid legal confrontations even if, from the firm's perspective, the dismissal is justified.

The aggregate direct costs of wrongful-termination litigation may not reflect potential risks if firms are avoiding litigation by engaging in preventative activities. These activities can be very expensive and need to be considered in any comprehensive accounting of the costs of the evolving employer liabilities. Most directly, firms can avoid the legal threat by not firing workers even when justified by economic conditions or poor job performance. Business might be reluctant to expand employment in response to changing product demand or other exogenous factors which increase the short-run need for labor input. The firm might adjust the employee mix, trading off production efficiency for diminished exposure to liability. Younger workers with short employment histories and unreliable references could be more risky. Older workers, despite their experience, might also be risky because of the higher sums they are awarded by juries. Changes in the utilization of overtime hours, part-time employees, or temporary workers are also possible. Managers might be reluctant to engage in risky ventures such as new product development or market expansion, out of fear of being left with a surplus of workers that can be terminated only at great expense. Firms would be prone not to adopt new technologies that displace labor in favor of capital equipment.

In addition to decisions that affect the utilization of labor, firms can avoid liability by changing the process of decisionmaking. Carefully screening potential employees, conducting extensive interviews, tracking down references, and maintaining rigorous qualifying standards diminish the risks of hiring the wrong person. Of course, this process is costly and could arbitrarily screen out higher risk persons with lots of potential. In addition to changes in hiring practices, firms will formalize the performance review, evaluation, promotion, and compensation process. Human-resource decisionmaking will become centralized, hierarchical, and systematic. Individuals will have less autonomy in personnel matters as internal mechanisms emerge for the purpose of exerting organizational oversight and risk management.

The decision to terminate an employee will no longer come at the discretion of immediate supervisors. Instead, grounds for termination will need to be well-documented and reviewed by senior executives, corporate counsel, and human resource specialists. Some firms will adopt an internal adjudication process for resolving workplace disputes without relying on the legal system. Decisions will be rendered by individuals perceived as having few vested interests in the disposition of the dispute.

The fact that many firms voluntarily provide implicit job guarantees and organize internal mechanisms to protect workers from unjust treatment, even in the absence of legal pressures, suggests that the marginal effects of employee protection might be less significant. For example, many businesses organized institutionalized procedures for ensuring fair treatment of personnel long before the erosion of employment at will. In many corporations, even nonunion employees can air grievances and appeal the decisions of supervisors. Although the 1988 Worker Adjustment and Retraining Notification Act mandates that some employers must provide workers 60 days advance notice of layoffs, recent studies of this legislation's effect suggest that workers are typically aware of impending employment reductions, even without formal notification requirements.

When workforce reductions are inevitable because of changing economic conditions or technological changes, firms frequently attempt to smooth the transition of displaced workers. Although lifetime employment is not feasible when long-run economic survival is at stake, the neoclassical caricature of the ruthless, profit-maximizing firm making instantaneous adjustments to the workforce does not represent reality. Firms are reluctant to lay off workers, preferring to rely on natural attrition, retraining, buyouts, and early retirement to achieve the desired level of employment.

Of course, such seemingly altruistic behavior does not imply that firms are not concerned with their long-run profitability. To begin with, there can be little doubt that a firm's treatment of a subset of its employees will affect the morale, loyalty, and productivity of remaining workers. Surely, a history of unfair labor practices will affect the ability to recruit high-quality employees in the future. Also, the reputation that a firm has a voluntary commitment to "fair" employment practices, though not providing an absolute lifetime guarantee, certainly reduces the expected probability that any given employee will lose his or her job. Since workers value such job security, firms will be able to pay lower wage rates in return for less flexibility in reducing the workforce. This has the potential for making both firms and workers better off. Finally, the higher probability of a long job tenure will induce workers to invest in training human capital that is firm-specific in nature.

4. STATUTORY REGULATION OF EMPLOYMENT SECURITY

Page 958. Please add the following to note 1.

See Cecil v. Cardinal Drilling Co., 244 Mont. 405, 797 P.2d 232 (1990) (executive discharged from oil drilling company during period of decline in oil prices was discharged for a legitimate business reason).

Chapter 11

UNEMPLOYMENT

A. BANKRUPTCY

2. PRIORITY FOR ADMINISTRATIVE EXPENSES

Page 985. Please add the following note.

2. By classifying the pension benefits as prepetition contingent claims rather than postpetition administrative priority claims, the court in In re Chateaugay Corp., 130 B.R. 690 (S.D.N.Y.1991), significantly reduced the funds available to pension beneficiaries.

In a bankruptcy reorganization, it is expected that postpetition or administrative claims will be paid 100 cents on the dollar and that unsecured, prepetition (non-priority) claims will receive significantly less, sometimes as low as 20–25 cents on the dollar.

Is that result equitable?

B. PLANT CLOSINGS

Page 998. Please add the following to the Note on Federal Plant–Closing Law.

For judicial construction of WARN, see Jones v. Kayser–Roth Hosiery, Inc., 748 F.Supp. 1292 (E.D.Tenn.1990), amended 753 F.Supp. 218 (1990). See also Hotel Employees Restaurant Employees International Union Local 54 v. Elsinore Shore Associates, 768 F.Supp. 1117 (D.N.J. 1991) (WARN does not apply when Casino Control Commission and not the employer ordered the closing of the casino).

E. UNEMPLOYMENT INSURANCE

3. LEGAL ISSUES IN UNEMPLOYMENT INSURANCE

Page 1037. Please add the following to note 1.

A Pennsylvania court found no violation of the Free Exercise Clause of the First Amendment when a parochial school teacher, dismissed for violating church doctrine, was denied unemployment benefits because of her misconduct in marrying a non-Catholic man previously divorced from a Catholic woman. Bishop Leonard Regional Catholic School v. Unemployment Compensation Board of Review, 140 Pa.Cmwlth. 428, 593 A.2d 28 (1991).

Page 1037.   Please add the following to note 2.

Under the willful misconduct standard, the Supreme Court of Montana held that an employee must show "intentional disregard of the employer's expectation." Negligence will not suffice to cut off unemployment benefits. LaVe v. Montana State Department of Labor & Industry, 239 Mont. 339, 780 P.2d 189 (1989).

Page 1039.   Please add the following to note 8.

An employee who refused to submit to a urine test did not commit misconduct preventing the award of unemployment compensation where the employer's demand for the test was unreasonable under the circumstances. The court upheld the agency's finding that the demand was unreasonable because the corporation had no official policy in place on drug testing and had relied solely on the unsubstantiated allegations of a hostile employee as the basis for its demand. Employment Security Commission v. Western Gas Processors, Ltd., 786 P.2d 866 (Wyo. 1990).

Page 1039.   Please add the following note.

9. A truck driver, whose prior terrible driving record made him uninsurable, was terminated by his employer. The court found that the employee's uninsurability did not constitute misconduct, thereby reversing the denial of unemployment benefits. Otero v. New Mexico Employment Security Division, 109 N.M. 412, 785 P.2d 1031 (1990).

Page 1045.   Please add the following note.

8. In McCourtney v. Imprimis Technology, Inc., 465 N.W.2d 721 (Minn.App.1991), the court found that persistent absences to care for a sick baby did not constitute misconduct and thus did not disqualify the employee from receiving unemployment benefits. "In light of McCourtney's good faith efforts, her inability to find care for her child is not 'misconduct' within the meaning of [the Minnesota statute.]" See also Mississippi Employment Security Commission v. Bell, 584 So.2d 1270 (Miss.1991) (recent absenteeism of long-term reliable employee due to difficulty in finding someone to take her children to school did not constitute misconduct).

Is it fair to the employer to require unemployment benefits in such cases? In the absence of inexpensive, reliable child care, is there any other option?

4. THE POLICY DEBATE

Page 1061.   Please delete the Schlozman & Verba article and insert the following.

GARY BURTLESS, IS UNEMPLOYMENT INSURANCE READY FOR THE 1990s?, SOCIAL INSURANCE ISSUES FOR THE NINETIES: PROCEEDINGS OF THE THIRD CONFERENCE OF THE NATIONAL ACADEMY OF SOCIAL INSURANCE
164–174 (Paul N. Van De Water, ed. 1992).

Effects of Unemployment Insurance

What are the wider effects of the system? Unemployment insurance offers vital income protection to experienced workers who become jobless because of involuntary layoff. In spite of the crucial economic role the program plays, it suffers from a shameful reputation among some economists, journalists, and policymakers. It has such a reputation because unemployment benefits can prolong spells of joblessness. Workers collecting a weekly unemployment check may not devote as much time or effort to finding a new job as workers who do not collect benefits. Even more important, insured workers may reject a job offer that an uninsured worker would accept because the income cushion UI provides permits the insured to be choosier. Economists like to say that these behavioral effects of unemployment insurance represent adverse incentives of the program.

Policymakers were aware of adverse incentives when they designed the current system. To reduce the influence of these incentives, federal and state legislatures imposed two important conditions on insurance. First, benefits are paid only to unemployed workers who can demonstrate that they are available for and actively seeking work. This requirement gives rise to the mountains of forms that jobless workers are now asked to fill out in order to receive benefits. Second, benefits are denied to workers who reject an offer of suitable employment (meaning a job roughly equivalent to the job that was lost). These two conditions are notoriously difficult to enforce in practice, so the American system of unemployment insurance possesses one other notable feature: Benefits are generally limited to twenty-six weeks. Unemployment beyond that is not ordinarily compensated in this country. By international standards, this period of protection is very brief. Virtually all other industrialized countries offer at least a year of benefits, and in several countries the duration is much longer.

In spite of these limitations on American benefits, many economists and policymakers suspect that unemployment insurance contributes to the high level of unemployment we now suffer. A variety of analysts have examined the size of the adverse impacts of unemployment insurance and have concluded that more generous benefits do indeed lengthen the average duration of unemployment among insured workers. A good guess is that a 10 percent increase in weekly benefits prolongs the average spell of unemployment by around one week. A one-week increase in the potential duration of benefits (from, say, twenty-six weeks to twenty-seven weeks) would increase the average length of an insured unemployment spell by about one-tenth of a week, or perhaps a bit more. An honest assessment of jobless benefits must therefore conclude that some of the adverse consequences that economists worry about do in fact occur.

These adverse consequences do not take us very far, however, in explaining the current level and trend in national unemployment. Only about four in ten unemployed workers collect unemployment benefits, and nearly all of the insured became jobless because of a layoff that was in no way caused by the existence of the program. Thus, if insurance were eliminated tomorrow, the level of joblessness would fall only slightly. Furthermore, if some of the insured unemployed experience longer spells of unemployment because of the existence of the program, it must also be the case that some uninsured unemployed workers experience shorter spells because they are more likely to land a job that has been turned down by an insured unemployed worker. In a labor market with a long queue of workers seeking jobs, a job that is rejected by a worker collecting benefits will be promptly snapped up by a desparate uninsured worker.

More fundamentally, it is the goal of unemployment insurance to permit insured workers to reject unsuitable job offers. We provide jobless benefits in this country (as do other advanced industrialized economies) precisely because our workers must acquire costly skills that can often be applied only in specialized occupations or jobs. When workers lose these jobs because of a downturn in demand, it is advantageous for them and for the wider economy if they carefully seek out the best opportunity to apply their specialized skills. In an economy with two unemployed workers and two job vacancies, it is efficient to subsidize the two workers to sort themselves into the job openings so that their skills are put to best use and their joint earnings are maximized. The two workers benefit and the wider economy gains if the best possible match is made between workers and vacancies. Furthermore, the insurance protection provided under UI encourages workers to undertake investments in specialized skills that otherwise might be regarded as excessively risky. On balance, I think that some economists (and most op-ed writers at the *Wall Street Journal*) tend to exaggerate the adverse effects of unemployment insurance and ignore the vital function it plays in protecting skilled and semi-skilled workers against the hazards of job loss. Sadly, they also ignore the way it promotes efficiency.

Declining Unemployment Insurance Coverage

Whether the effects of unemployment insurance have been positive or negative, they have shrunk in recent years. In the 1980s, joblessness rose to new postwar highs, but the share of unemployed workers drawing unemployment benefits fell to new lows. The percentage of jobless workers collecting benefits has risen modestly in the past couple of years, but still remains well below the levels prevailing before the mid–1980s.

The proportion of the unemployed collecting benefits declined for several reasons. First and most important, fewer unemployed workers now apply for benefits when they lose their jobs. In part, the drop in applications is due to a change in eligibility requirements for unemployment insurance, which are established both at the state and the national levels. In addition, some unemployed workers may have decided against applying for benefits as the after-tax value of those benefits fell. Finally, the nature of unemployment has changed.

* * *

Extended Unemployment Insurance Benefits

The extended benefit UI program offers insurance protection beyond twenty-six weeks of unemployment for workers who have exhausted regular benefits and who live in states with high unemployment. The drop in the percentage of unemployed job losers collecting regular benefits has directly affected the insured unemployment rate (IUR), which serves as the basis for triggering extended UI benefits. If I am correct in estimating that the number of regular UI claimants has fallen one-fifth, then the IUR is also about one-fifth too low relative to the civilian or total unemployment rate (TUR), which provides a more accurate gauge of current labor market conditions.

The relationship between the insured and the total unemployment rates is shown in the two panels of figure 3. Although the IUR and TUR tend to move in parallel fashion over the business cycle, they have drifted apart since 1960. Before 1980, this drift could be easily explained by changing regulations about the insurance coverage of employed workers and by the changing composition of the civilian unemployed—who were younger, less likely to be job losers, and drawn more from industries with low levels of insurance coverage than their earlier counterparts. After 1980, however, the sharp decline in the IUR relative to the TUR has been due almost entirely to the sharp drop in the fraction of new job losers collecting benefits.

Figure 3
Insured Unemployment Rate
and Civilian Unemployment Rate, 1960–91

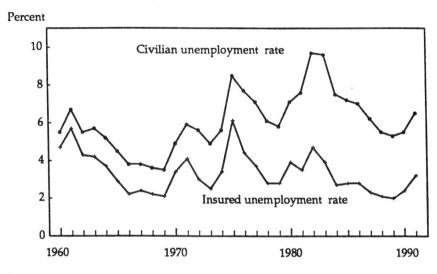

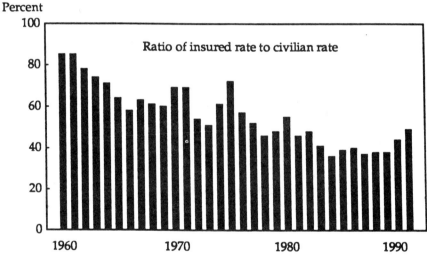

Source: U.S. Department of Labor, Employment and Training Administration.

[G11024]

As a result of the drop in the IUR, the extended benefit program has virtually ceased to function. Even with unemployment approaching 7 percent, only a handful of states offer extended benefits. When the employment situation in a state deteriorates, its total unemployment rate rises, but its insured unemployment rate often does not rise enough to trigger extended benefits. The result is that the extended benefit program either fails to be triggered or is triggered late in an economic downturn. Moreover, even when extended benefits become available, the IUR can be expected to fall below the critical threshold relatively early in an economic recovery. Many beneficiaries are thus dropped from the insurance rolls even though the local job market remains very weak.

The extended benefit program also contracted over the past decade because of significant changes in federal law passed in 1981. Before 1982, the extended benefit trigger rate was computed by including recipients of both regular and extended benefits in the count of insured unemployed. (Thus, the trigger rate used before 1982 was not identical to the IUR, which excludes recipients of extended benefits from the numerator.) Since extended benefit recipients are now excluded, the level of insured unemployment needed to keep the extended benefit program turned on has effectively been raised. Also, before 1981, the extended benefit program could be triggered in all states if the national trigger rate exceeded 4.5 percent. The national trigger rate was eliminated by the 1981 legislation. Beginning in October 1982, extended benefits have been available only in states in which the IUR exceeds 5 percent and is at least 120 percent of the rate over the previous two years. Some states also provide benefits when the IUR reaches 6 percent, regardless of the rate in previous years. These trigger rates are one percentage point higher than the comparable rates in effect before 1982.

The legislative reforms of 1981, along with the sharp drop in the number of regular UI claimants, had a calamitous effect on the extended benefit program. At the end of 1982, when the civilian unemployment rate reached 10.8 percent—a postwar record—only fourteen states with particularly high insured unemployment rates offered extended benefits. By October 1983, with unemployment still hovering above 9 percent, only two states and Puerto Rico offered extended benefits. In contrast, during the 1974–76 recession, when unemployment reached a high of 9.0 percent, all fifty states offered extended benefits for prolonged periods. As a practical matter, the extended benefit program no longer operates as an effective countercyclical stabilizer. Except in extraordinarily severe recessions, the program is unlikely to offer benefits to a sizable number of workers.

Policy Implications

An important implication of these developments is that the unemployment insurance system has become a much weaker source of countercyclical stimulus during economic downturns. The effectiveness of the extended benefit program has been cut at least in half as a result of the legislative changes passed in 1981 and the continued weakness of the IUR as a measure of the labor market situation. The stimulus provided by the regular twenty-six-week program has dropped one-fifth because of the decline in the number of claimants relative to the number of unemployed job losers. And the stimulus provided under both the regular and the extended benefit programs has dropped an additional 15 to 20 percent as a result of the taxation of benefits. In comparison with the level of countercyclical stimulus available during the 1960s and 1970s, the stimulus provided by the current system has dropped at least a third. The income protection available to jobless workers has dropped a similar proportion.

Chapter 12

RETIREMENT

B. MANDATORY RETIREMENT

Page 1084. Please add the following to note 11.

In Hebert v. Mohawk Rubber Co., 872 F.2d 1104 (1st Cir.1989), the court held that "absent the option to choose to keep working under lawful conditions, an employer's offer of a choice between early retirement with benefits or discharge without benefits is nothing other than a discharge."

C. PRIVATE PENSIONS

4. ERISA

Page 1108. Please add the following case before subpart b.

IN RE CHATEAUGAY CORP.
945 F.2d 1205 (2d Cir.1991), cert. denied 112 S.Ct. 1167 (1992).

MESKILL, CIRCUIT JUDGE:

This is an appeal from a judgment of the United States District Court for the Southern District of New York, affirming a judgment of the United States Bankruptcy Court. The bankruptcy court, in orders dated August 1 and 4, 1988, concluded that the Retiree Benefits Bankruptcy Protection Act of 1988, did not require LTV Steel Company, BCNR Mining Corporation, Nemacolin Mines Corporation and Tuscaloosa Energy Corporation (collectively, with LTV Steel, "LTV") to continue to pay health benefits to their retirees. The bankruptcy court also concluded that the United Mine Workers of America 1974 Benefit Plan and Trust (Benefit Trust) was responsible for the continued payment of retiree health benefits. ...

We conclude that the Bankruptcy Protection Act does not require LTV to continue payment of the retiree benefits herein at issue. The three mining operations have ceased doing business, the collectively bargained 1984 National Bituminous Coal Wage Agreement (1984 Wage Agreement) has expired, and the continued provision of the retiree health benefits by the Benefit Trust was expressly considered under the 1984 Wage Agreement. We therefore affirm the decision of the district court. ...

120

LTV filed for bankruptcy under Chapter 11 and has not obtained dismissal of the case or approval of any plan of reorganization under section 1129. LTV was still paying benefits on October 2, 1986, the date that triggered the application of the Act. Based on these facts, the Benefit Trust asserts that LTV must continue to pay the retiree benefits until a plan of reorganization is approved. We disagree.

The Act expressly states that the trustee in bankruptcy, here LTV, the debtor-in-possession, must continue to "pay benefits to retired former employees under a plan, fund, or program maintained or established by the debtor prior to filing a petition [for bankruptcy]." Thus, we must analyze the "plan, fund, or program maintained or established" by LTV before it filed for bankruptcy in order to determine the trustee's obligation to LTV's retired former employees. ...

In sum, the Mining Companies were obligated to pay retiree benefits under the terms of the Wage Agreement. The Benefit Trust was to pay benefits if the Mining Companies were no longer in business. No provision in the agreement discusses coverage upon the expiration of the Wage Agreement without adoption of a subsequent agreement. The Benefits Trust contends that because LTV, as parent to the signatory Mining Companies, is not "out of business" under the narrow definition set forth in the 1984 Wage Agreement, LTV must continue to pay the retiree benefits during LTV's reorganization.

There are several factors militating against this interpretation. Section 10 of the General Description of the Health and Retirement Benefits, under the heading "Health Care," in Article XX, states "health care benefits are guaranteed during the term of this Agreement subject to the terms of this Agreement at the level of benefits provided in the 1950 Benefit Plan, the 1974 Benefit Plan, and the Employer Benefit Plan." This portion of the Wage Agreement suggests that the parties are bound by the provisions of the Wage Agreement only as long as the Wage Agreement itself is effective.

The expiration date of the 1984 Wage Agreement was clearly set forth in Article XXIX. It states in pertinent part:

> Except as provided in Article XXVIII, section (b) (Severability Clause), this Agreement shall not be subject to termination by either party signatory hereto prior to 11:59 p.m., January 31, 1988 provided, however, that either the parties of the first part or the party of the second part may terminate this Agreement on or after 11:59 p.m., January 31, 1988 by giving at least sixty days written notice to the other party of such desired termination date.

The language of the above quoted provisions indicates that once LTV terminated the Wage Agreement upon its expiration in 1988, health benefits were no longer guaranteed under the Wage Agreement. There is no intimation that the parties intended LTV's obligation to continue beyond the life of the Wage Agreement. LTV notified the employees of the Mining Companies that it would cease operations without continuance in 1986. LTV notified the Benefit Trust in November and again in December of 1988 that the 1984 Wage Agreement would terminate after January 31, 1988. The 1984 Wage Agreement ceased to be effective after that date. Thus the parties were no longer bound by it as of that date. If LTV is not bound by the terms of the Wage Agreement, LTV has no obligation to pay the retiree health benefits. The Benefit Trust points to no other agreement or provision within the 1984 Wage Agreement that would suggest a contrary result.

Based on the analysis set forth above, the "plan, fund, or program maintained or established" by the Mining Companies at the time LTV sought protection from creditors under Chapter 11 can be described simply. The Mining Companies guaranteed payment of retiree benefits during the term of the Wage Agreement. The Wage Agreement expired immediately after January 31, 1988. Regardless of the obligations of any other parties, neither the Mining Companies nor LTV Steel were obliged to pay retiree benefits after the termination of the Wage Agreement. The 1984 Wage Agreement was the plan in effect at the time LTV sought protection under Chapter 11. The Bankruptcy Protection Act requires that during reorganization the parties continue to provide benefits according to the plan in effect at the time of the declaration of bankruptcy; the Bankruptcy Protection Act does not alter the terms of that plan. As noted, the plan does not require LTV to pay for benefits after the 1984 Wage Agreement expired. LTV Steel and the Mining Companies, therefore, are not obligated by the Wage Agreement or by statute to continue to pay for retiree benefits. The Benefit Trust has conceded that if it is determined that LTV is not required to pay the retiree health benefits the Benefit Trust is so required. ...

Here the retired employees are guaranteed provision of health benefits for life under the collective bargaining agreement. That agreement has been interpreted to mean that if the Wage Agreement terminates, the benefits are still provided but they are provided by the Benefit Trust, instead of by the companies. The Mining Companies ceased operations in 1986. The 1984 Wage Agreement expired in 1988. Upon its expiration, the burden for the provision of retiree health benefits shifted to the Benefit Trust. There is no cessation of benefits, there is no termination of benefits. Whether the plan is able to fund fully the benefits is a separate issue. The retired employees are receiving exactly what they bargained for in the 1984 Wage Agreement. ...

RESTANI, JUDGE: I dissent.

According to the plain language of section 3 of the Retiree Benefits Bankruptcy Protection Act of 1988, "the trustee shall pay [health] benefits to retired former employees under a plan, fund, or program maintained or established by the debtor prior to filing a petition, ... until ... the dismissal of the case involved; or ... the effective date of a plan confirmed under section 1129 ...." The Act also provides that the level of benefits may be modified if there is an agreement on modification, or the bankruptcy court finds modification is necessary to reorganization and "the balance of equities clearly favors the modification."

The district court decided, in essence, that although the Act applies to health benefits that are terminable at will, it does not apply to health benefits that are provided pursuant to a contract obligation which is interpreted to have expired. I would reverse this decision as I do not find any intent on the part of Congress to distinguish between a contract right which never existed and one which terminated. ...

The legislative history cited by the district court and, more extensively, by the majority, is consistent with the plain language of the Act. The district court and majority, however, have seized upon the concept of the "unilateral" nature of certain terminations of benefits, a concept found in the Heinz statement quoted supra. This reliance is misplaced. Under the facts at hand, LTV's decision not to continue its 1984 Wage Agreement obligations to the retirees was no less unilateral than the decision to terminate "at will" benefits, and certainly LTV's original attempt to reject the Wage Agreement pursuant to the trustee's ordinary bankruptcy powers was a unilateral action. But even more persuasive is the absence of the limiting word against unilateral termination of benefits, but the plain language of the statute does not limit it to this purpose only. As explained by the sponsors of the legislation, the Act applies whether or not a collective bargaining agreement is in effect. "The provisions of section 3 apply to union and nonunion retirees .... Benefits subject to these standards are not required to arise from a collective bargaining agreement." 134 Cong.Rec. 12,698 (1988) (statement of Sen. Metzenbaum). "This legislation protects retired employees who are covered by a collective bargaining agreement, as well as those where no collective bargaining agreement is in effect." 133 Cong.Rec. 21,099 (1987) (statement of Sen. Heflin). ...

Accordingly, the Act continues all retiree health benefits which are in effect immediately prior to bankruptcy. The Act also states that termination or modification of benefits is not permitted prior to reorganization unless either the trustee and an authorized representative of the affected parties agree to the modification, or if the trustee convinces the court that such modification is necessary and equitable. The clear purpose of the Act is to give the bankruptcy court power to resolve the competing interests of retirees, debtors and creditors, if agreement as to continuation and level of benefits cannot be reached. The health benefits of retirees are not to be terminated by any action until the bankruptcy court has time to act. The passages of legislative history cited by the majority do not reveal an intent other than that reflected in the plain language of the statute; that is, despite contractual rights or lack thereof, benefits are to continue on an interim basis until the parties agree or until the bankruptcy court makes the determinations specified in the Act. If Congress intended some distinction between former employees without contracts and those whose contractual rights had expired, it simply did not say so. If it had any distinction among employees in mind, it was a distinction between employees of companies which seek protection under the bankruptcy laws and employees of companies who do not. I believe that the majority errs in reading into the statute special exemptions applicable to bargained for benefits, not enunciated by Congress.

I believe the majority also erred in relying in any way on the presence of the Benefit Trust with regard to interpretation of the statute. The Benefit Trust is intended as a last resort for the funding of retiree health benefits. Royal Coal II finds the Benefit Trust liable, despite contract language to the contrary, because of the overall purpose of the contract, that is, retirees must be provided for. Here, the act spells out how provision for retirees is to be made. Moreover, although successor Wage Agreements require funding of the Benefit Trust to meet retiree health benefit requirements, it has not been established that current and future signatories will be able to bear the burden of former signatories throughout the lifetimes of the retirees. This factual issue is not resolved. In any case, given the plain language of the statute, I would find the status of the Benefit Trust irrelevant as to statutory construction.

I do not reach the issue of the contractual liability of the Benefit Trust. If LTV remains obligated to pay benefits under the statutory criteria, the obligation of the Benefit Trust does not arise. The bankruptcy court has not made the findings which would resolve this issue.

Note

One implication for pension beneficiaries of the holding in *Chateaugay* is that companies can contractually reserve the right to terminate pension benefits. Another implication is that no matter what the contractual language, benefits end when the contract does. Is this consistent with 11 U.S.C. § 1114? Would you support new legislation?

Page 1134. Please add the following to note 5.

See Jess v. Pandick, Inc., 699 F.Supp. 698 (N.D.Ill.1988) (constructive discharge will state a claim under ERISA).

Page 1139. Please add the following to note 1.

In 1981, Michigan enacted a law allowing coordination of workers' compensation benefits with employer-funded pension plan payments.

Workers injured before the effective date of the statute were subjected to these provisions, prompting some concern about the legality of the changes. In 1987, the Michigan legislature passed a law which clearly indicated that the coordination of benefits provision of the 1981 law was not intended to reduce benefits for injuries occurring before the 1981 law's enactment.

Michigan employers contended that the 1987 law violated their constitutional rights under the Due Process and Contract Clauses of the state and federal constitutions by retroactively altering the level of benefits due and payable prior to the amendment. The Michigan Supreme Court, and later the United States Supreme Court, upheld the 1987 law. Romein v. General Motors Corp., 436 Mich. 515, 462 N.W.2d 555 (1990), affirmed 112 S.Ct. 1105 (1992).

Page 1139. Please add the following to note 2.

The first wife of a deceased pension plan participant brought an action to declare the decedent's second wife disqualified from receiving benefits under the plan on the ground of her conviction for manslaughter of the decedent. The district court held that New York law prohibiting a killer from profiting from her crime is not preempted by ERISA. Mendez–Bellido v. Board of Trustees, 709 F.Supp. 329 (E.D.N.Y.1989).

Page 1142. Please add the following note.

9. State law fraud and misrepresentation claims brought by early retirees who allegedly relied on their employer's misleading statements about planned future increases in an early retirement package when they retired are preempted by ERISA, even though the statute provides no remedy. Lee v. E.I. DuPont de Nemours & Co., 894 F.2d 755 (5th Cir.1990).

Page 1150. Please add the following notes before Subpart 5.

Note on Pension Beneficiary Bankruptcy

In Shumate v. Patterson, 943 F.2d 362 (4th Cir.1991), cert. granted 112 S.Ct. 932 (1992), the Supreme Court is deciding whether Congress intended for ERISA protection to end when a beneficiary of a pension plan goes bankrupt. Four circuit courts have held that qualified ERISA pension and profit sharing plans are exempt from the bankruptcy estate under 11 U.S.C. § 541(c)(2). Four other circuit courts have held that Congress intended to include virtually all of a debtor's property interests in the estate. The result will determine whether an individual's pension plan is part of the estate and therefore available to satisfy creditors' claims or whether the pension plan holder risks losing the pension on filing for bankruptcy. See also In re Doskocil Companies Inc., 130 B.R. 870 (Bkrtcy.Kan.1991) (Chapter 11 debtor has no obligation to continue health and life insurance benefits under plan which allowed amendment, modification or termination of benefits).

Note on Company Pension Obligations in a Liquidation

The Retiree Benefits Act of 1988 was enacted as a result of the bankruptcy by steel multinational LTV and the LTV Corporation's decision to terminate the health and insurance benefits of its retirees upon the filing of the Chapter 11 petition. Even though the Bankruptcy Court provisionally restored the payments to the retirees, Congress enacted legislation to codify the requirement that Chapter 11 debtors continue to pay retiree benefits. 11 U.S.C. § 1114(b)(2).

The enactment of the Retiree Benefits Act had a profound impact on the way courts looked at the priority that all benefits, including pension plans, must receive if a company goes bankrupt. Often, when the Retiree Committee of a corporation in Chapter 11 petitions the court for priority against other creditors, the trustees file cross motions claiming economic hardship.

Absent "Congressional consensus that retirees in liquidating cases should be entitled to greater protections," the court in *Eastern* stated, "the courts will not grant them." In some of the recent mega bankruptcies, often the result is delays or decreases in retiree payments. At the time of the Eastern Airlines shutdown, 10,000 retirees were receiving benefits of $3.6 million per month.

IN RE IONOSPHERE CLUBS, INC., EASTERN AIR LINES, INC.
134 B.R. 515 (Bkrtcy.S.D.N.Y.1991).

Burton R. Lifland:

Before the Court is a motion brought by the Official Retiree Committee ("Retiree Committee") appointed pursuant to 11 U.S.C. § 1114(b)(2) seeking a declaration that 11 U.S.C. § 1114 gives retiree claims a broad all encompassing administrative claim status, and a cross motion in opposition by Martin R. Shugrue, Chapter 11 Trustee ("Trustee") for Eastern Airlines ("Eastern" or "Debtor"), joined by the Official Creditors' Committee with separate pleadings seeking to limit the administrative status of those claims.

Eastern, a major public air carrier operating under the aegis of its Chapter 11 Trustee, ceased revenue flying on January 19, 1991 and began an orderly liquidation program which remains ongoing. There is no possibility of rehabilitation. At the time the Trustee shut down the airline, there were approximately 10,000 retirees under age sixty-five receiving benefits from Eastern at a level of approximately $3.6 million per month. The benefits continued at that level until modified in May of this year pursuant to the procedures called for under § 1114, a relatively recent addition to Chapter 11 of the Bankruptcy Code ("Code"). ...

Earlier in this case, the Trustee commenced negotiations for modification of retiree benefits with the Retiree Committee which had been appointed on April 2, 1991 to represent (1) Retirees under collective bargaining agreements with the Air Line Pilots Association, International ("ALPA"); and (2) "Non–Contract" retirees, made up of non-union management and clerical retirees. Retirees represented by the International Association of Machinists and Aerospace Workers, AFL–CIO ("IAM") and retirees represented by the Transport Workers Union of America, AFL–CIO, Local 553 ("TWU") were and continue to be represented by their respective unions ("IAM", "TWU" or "Unions"). The negotiations among the Trustee, Retiree Committee and the Unions continued pending a May 22, 1991 hearing scheduled to consider the Trustee's motion for relief under § 1114(g) or for an interim relief ruling under § 1114(h). On the day of the hearing, the Retiree Committee and the Trustee reached an interim agreement covering the period from July 1, 1991 through December 31, 1991 (the "Interim Agreement"). The IAM, TWU and the Trustee were unable to come to an agreement. Consequently, the Trustee proceeded with the § 1114(h) motion for interim relief and, at the conclusion of the hearing, was authorized to impose interim modifications on the union retirees. Such modifications were substantially identical to those agreed to by the Retiree Committee. ...

POSITION OF THE PARTIES

A. Retiree Committee.

Asserting a plethora of theories in support of an overarching administrative claim for unaccrued future benefits as well as those due to modification, the Retiree Committee has asked this Court to find that retiree benefits enjoy a super-priority such that: (1) regardless of whether Eastern liquidates in Chapter 11 or Chapter 7, the priority afforded to retiree benefits by § 1114 protects all Eastern retiree benefits to the extent unencumbered funds are available; (2) by virtue of unrejected collective bargaining agreements, Eastern pilot retirees have unalterable priority rights under Bankruptcy Code § 1113; and (3) post-petition retiree claims are entitled to priority as administrative expenses of Eastern's Chapter 11 estate under § 503(b)(1).

B. Trustee.

The Trustee has asked this court to find that: (1) Retiree Benefits Lost due to modification under § 1114 are prepetition general unsecured claims; (2) the retiree's claims for benefits will be prepetition general unsecured claims in the event Eastern's case is converted from a case under Chapter 11 to a case under Chapter 7; (3) § 1114 is the exclusive means by which the Trustee must pay and modify benefits; and (4) independent of § 1114, the retirees' claims for benefits are prepetition general unsecured claims.

C. Creditors' Committee.

In addition to joining the Trustee's arguments, the Creditors' Committee has asked this court to find that: (1) pursuant to the terms of the agreements granting benefits, Eastern has the right to terminate retiree benefits without giving rise to any claims whatsoever; and (2) § 1114 is inapplicable in a liquidating case.

PROCEDURE FOR MODIFICATION OR TERMINATION OF BENEFITS: THE RELATIONSHIP BETWEEN §§ 1113 AND 1114

The parties dispute whether § 1114 is the exclusive provision of Chapter 11 governing modification of retiree benefits. There is no statutory provision answering this question, and there is no legislative history that provides an unequivocal answer . . . .

Thus, without any clear indication from Congress, the courts are left to resolve this issue through principles of statutory construction. It is well settled that "where there is no clear intention otherwise, a specific statute will not be controlled or nullified by a general one, regardless of the priority of enactment." Application of this principle here leads to the conclusion that § 1114 is the exclusive provision relating to the modification or termination of retiree benefits. § 1114 specifically and unequivocally addresses retiree issues that are otherwise generally covered by § 1113. . . .

At this point, the Retiree Committee is the only representative authorized to negotiate with the Trustee for the modification or termination of retiree benefits under any section of the Bankruptcy Code. ALPA, the union bargaining unit, cannot negotiate retiree benefits after electing not to represent the pilot retirees under § 1114. Once ALPA opted out of retiree representation, its ability to do so was extinguished. Applying a § 1113 collective bargaining agreement rejection process would restore the potentially conflicted ALPA back into the negotiation process. This is antithetical to the statutory scheme which clearly contemplates that the Trustee will negotiate retiree modification issues with the authorized representative of the union retirees solely within the confines of § 1114. . . .

NON–APPLICABILITY OF § 1114 IN CHAPTER 7

The Trustee's motion requests a determination that upon expiration of the stipulation of the parties that modified benefits through December 31, 1991, the retiree claims for benefits will be prepetition general unsecured claims in the event Eastern's case is converted from a case under Chapter 11 to a case under Chapter 7. The Trustee has not disputed that without any further modification or conversion to Chapter 7, such claims will be administrative expense claims. The Trustee has made clear that with respect to retiree issues he intends to either modify or terminate the benefits under Chapter 11 or propose conversion of the case to Chapter 7.

In response, the Retiree Committee argues that conversion to Chapter 7 would not affect the status of the retiree claims. The Retiree Committee takes the position that the language of 11 U.S.C. § 1114(e)— "Notwithstanding any other provision of this title"—means that this provision applies over all other provisions of the Code. Alternatively, it argues that the filing of a Chapter 11 petition triggers § 1114; the provision then continues to establish a priority even if the case is later converted to Chapter 7. The Retiree Committe argues that this is so whether or not § 1114 would apply to a case that was originally filed under Chapter 7. This would be tantamount to the creation of a new elevated form of super-priority which, for want of a better label, I would call an adhesion priority. If Congress' intent was to make § 1114 priorities applicable in non-Chapter 11 cases, it would have placed coordinating amendments in either Chapter 1, 3, or 5. Chapter 11 provisions do not apply in Chapter 7. No court has held that § 1114 is applicable to a Chapter 7 case regardless of the circumstances. Therefore, only while a debtor is in Chapter 11 are those § 1114 mandated benefit payments administrative expenses. Once a Chapter 11 case is converted to a case under Chapter 7, retiree benefits are no longer mandated and can only be considered under the well established distributive scheme of the non-Chapter 11 chapters.

Accordingly, the conclusion is inescapable that § 1114 is not applicable in Chapter 7.

APPLICABILITY OF § 1114 IN CHAPTER 11 LIQUIDATING CASES

Because § 1114 is a relatively new statute reacting to recently heightened social concerns, this Court is faced with a situation which bankruptcy courts have only just begun to encounter and none have facilely resolved in the reported cases—that of deciding how § 1114 applies to a debtor that is effectively in liquidation, although it remains in Chapter 11. A review of the legislative history in the following sections reveals no indication that Congress ever contemplated that § 1114 would apply in a liquidating case. Nevertheless, it is an unrestrained provision in Chapter 11 and cannot be ignored.

The Retiree Benefits Protection Act of 1988 (Retiree Benefits Act) brought two additions to the Bankruptcy Code, § 1114 and § 1129(a)(13). Section 1114 provides the standards that must be followed before retiree benefits may be modified. Section 1129(a)(13) establishes that as a condition to confirmation, the plan must provide retiree benefits at the level established under § 1114 for the duration the debtor has obligated itself.

It is well known that the Retiree Benefits Act was enacted by Congress in response to the mammoth steel manufacturing LTV Corporation's short lived unilateral termination of the health and life insurance benefits of its retirees upon the filing of its Chapter 11 petition.

Almost immediately after the termination, this Court provisionally ordered restoration of the payments. Nevertheless, in response to LTV's actions, Congress enacted broad legislation to address the issue of a reorganizing debtor's obligation to continue paying retiree benefits during the pendency of the Chapter 11 reorganization. Unfortunately, as is obvious from the legislative history, in enacting § 1114, Congress reacted with expressed concern for the plight of retirees on the facts presented in LTV, and failed to specifically address issues relating to retiree benefits in other circumstances which arise, not atypically, in cases pending under Chapter 11 (i.e., liquidations or cases where there are no unencumbered assets available to pay retiree benefits, etc.). ...

A consistent premise underlying § 1114 is that a reorganization is in progress. This "necessary to permit the reorganization of the debtor" criterion is "robbed of its meaning" when the debtor is engaged in a liquidation. ...

In most reorganizations, the debtor in possession is confronted with the question of how to cut costs and increase profitability in furtherance of a successful rehabilitative reorganization effort. Congress drafted § 1114 to insure that debtors did not seek to effect reorganizations "on the back of retirees" for the benefit of other parties in interest. Section 1114 provides a status quo safeguard to retirees during the plan negotiation process. It requires a debtor to pay in a timely fashion and refrain from modifying any retiree benefits until a determination is made as to what modifications are "necessary to permit the reorganization of the debtor." This assumes that bargaining will facilitate that process that encourages the emergence of a viable entity from bankruptcy court. Conversely, in the Eastern case, the current lack of viability precludes any available income stream from which to pay retiree benefits or to swell a finite asset pool.

Since there are no material differences between the mechanics of liquidation in Chapter 11 or Chapter 7, Congress could not have intended the results of such liquidations to differ so markedly by enhancing the claim of retirees in one instance (a Chapter 11 liquidation) but not the other (a Chapter 7 liquidation). Accordingly, where the debtor is completely liquidating its assets in Chapter 11 in contemplation of a final distribution to creditors, that debtor should not be compelled to continue paying retiree benefits, in full, on a priority basis.

Applying § 1114 as requested by the Retiree Committee to liquidating Chapter 11 cases involving a large work force, in most instances, can result in the depletion of all, or substantially all of an estate's assets. In many cases, there would be insufficient funds even to pay administration creditors to complete the liquidation, and little or no funds for distribution to other general unsecured creditors. Such a result would be in violation of the overall objectives of the Bankruptcy

Code to pursue the greatest benefit for all creditors of the estate and to promote a fair and equitable distribution. ...

While the foregoing demonstrates the incompatibility of § 1114 as drafted when applied to a liquidation, absent corrective or clarifying legislation, the statute's placement in Chapter 11 requires its application to liquidating Chapter 11 cases.

APPLICATION OF § 1114 TO EASTERN'S CASE

In applying § 1114, it is incumbent upon this Court to reach an equitable result by deciphering Congressional design from what is clearly reactive legislation designed to address situations similar to those in the LTV bankruptcy. The Retiree Committee suggests that once a company gives up hope of reorganizing as a viable entity, retiree benefits can no longer be modified. This is so, it argues, because the applicable test for modification—"necessary to permit the reorganization of the debtor"—cannot be met. To interpret the quoted language in this fashion would imply that as a company is struggling to revitalize and conditions become increasingly bleak, the debtor would be entitled to progressively greater and greater modifications of its retiree benefits. Theoretically, at some point, the only way to salvage the reorganization would be to completely terminate retiree benefits. If the motion to modify or terminate the benefits is not heard before any possibility of reorganization is lost, then according to the Retiree Committee, the trustee would be unable to meet this "necessary to" test and would, thereafter, have forfeited any opportunity to modify retiree benefits in any way. This Court cannot find that Congress intended such an anomalous result. ...

CONCLUSION

When confronting similar circumstances, Judge Bodoh wrote:

> Like Congress, this Court is aware of the harsh circumstances of the retirees who face the loss of their health insurance coverage. Indeed, this Court witnesses daily the hardships imposed upon all parties by the misfortunes which result in bankruptcy. But short of printing money, there is no way to see that all claims are paid in full. The Bankruptcy Code recognizes this reality and provides a method for dealing with it, and the best that this Court can do is see that all of the provisions of the Code are given effect. In the present case, this means that the Court has made its best effort to enforce § 1114 in accordance with the intent of Congress while still acting within the traditional context of the Bankruptcy Code and pursuing the greatest benefit for all creditors of this estate.

In re GF Corp., 115 B.R. at 585. In bankruptcy court, hardships are shared, not unloaded on particular groups. Without an unequivocal Congressional mandate, this Court cannot agree that the retiree committee is entitled to the overwhelming super-priority they seek.

Through remedial legislation, the retirees have received some preferential treatment. In granting additional rights denied other unsecured creditors, Congress did not eschew the principle that retirees could share at least some of the burdens and disappointment that other parties experience in bankruptcy. If there is a Congressional consensus that retirees in liquidating cases should be entitled to greater protections than those discussed here, it is incumbent upon Congress to enact statutes setting forth standards that are in harmony with existing law and policy.

The Retiree Committee has appealed to this court's sense of fairness and equity and asked it to broadly apply § 105, if necessary, to provide a just result. There is no question that these claimants arouse a special sense of compassion. It is also inescapable that through § 1114, Congress has sought to establish a priority for retirees in bankruptcy cases that assures that they will receive a measure of enhanced treatment that is consistent with a bankruptcy court's role as a court of equity. In basic terms, § 1114 attempts to assure that retirees will receive their fair share. However, even in reorganization cases clearly governed by § 1114, it is not contemplated that retiree's will receive payment to the exclusion of all other unsecured creditors. Yet, that is the effect of the Retiree Committee's requests.

THEREFORE, THIS COURT HOLDS THAT:

(A) With respect to the Retiree Committee's motion: (1) to the extent that payments were made to retirees through June 30, 1991 under § 1114(e)(1), they are administrative expense claims; (2) to the extent payments are made through December 31, 1991 by stipulation of the parties and order of the Court, they are administrative expense claims; and (3) the motion is denied in all other respects.

(B) With respect to the Trustee's cross motion (joined by the Creditors' Committee): (1) absent corrective or clarifying legislation, § 1114 applies to liquidating Chapter 11 cases; (2) retiree benefits lost due to modification under § 1114 are prepetition general unsecured claims; (3) retiree claims for benefits that accrue after conversion to Chapter 7 are prepetition general unsecured claims; and (4) the present value of the prepetition retirees' claims for future benefits under (2) and (3) above is a prepetition general unsecured claims.

Notes and Questions

1. In *Eastern,* Chief Judge Lifland stated that, "In bankruptcy court, hardships are shared, not unloaded on particular groups. Without an unequivocal Congressional mandate, this court cannot agree that the retiree committee is entitled to the overwhelming super-priority they seek." Should retirees receive super-priority in bankruptcy? Is that what Congress intended?

2. In Senator Robert Dole's remarks, introducing the proposed Pension Security Act of 1992, he warned that "there is an estimated $40 billion in underfunded pensions, an increase of 25% from a year ago" and that "1991 witnessed the two largest claims in the history of PBGC when the pension plans of Pan American World Airways, underfunded by $900 million and Eastern Air Lines, underfunded by $700 million, were taken over."

The Dole bill proposed to protect pensions and the PBGC by (1) strengthening the minimum funding rules for underfunded plans; (2) providing additional incentives to fund pension promises and limit the PBGC's long-term liability; and (3) clarifying and improving the priority of PBGC's bankruptcy claims.

3. Ordinarily, a liquidation takes place when the debtor has filed bankruptcy under Chapter 7. (But see 11 U.S.C. § 1123(b)(4), which allows a debtor in a Chapter 11 case to file a liquidation plan.) Judge Lifland suggested that Congress did not consider pension issues in a liquidation case.

Senator Metzenbaum, the principal sponsor of 11 U.S.C. § 1114, stated that "reorganizing companies may never unilaterally cut off retiree insurance benefits [because] the burden of turning a company around should not rest on the backs of the retirees." But the court in *Eastern* found that "Congress did not contemplate that this legislation would impact debtors who were not in the process of reorganizing (i.e. not turning around).

Does this seem fair? Should pension benefits be given a priority in a Chapter 7 liquidation as well?

6. GOVERNMENT PENSIONS AS CONTRACT

Page 1162. Please add the following to note 5.

In Pineman v. Fallon, 662 F.Supp. 1311 (D.Conn.1987), the court held that the change in retirement age did not violate Contract Clause, Taking Clause, or Due Process rights under the United States Constitution for those employees who under prior law would have been entitled to such benefits. This decision was affirmed by the Second Circuit in Pineman v. Fallon, 842 F.2d 598 (2d Cir.1988), cert. denied 488 U.S. 824 (1988).

Page 1162. Please add the following note.

8. In one of the few challenges to divestment statutes, the Maryland Court of Appeals held that Baltimore's divestment ordinance did not impair the beneficiaries' contractual rights. In Board of Trustees v. Mayor of Baltimore City, 317 Md. 72, 562 A.2d 720 (1989), cert. denied 493 U.S. 1093 (1990), the court considered a challenge to ordinances requiring city pension funds to divest their holdings in companies doing

business in South Africa. The court noted that the law did not alter provisions establishing the level of benefits guaranteed to retirees. Even were the costs of divestiture to affect the retirement systems' profitability, the court found that such minimal costs would not unconstitutionally impair the obligations of contract—the lower court calculated that the initial divestiture would cost only $\frac{1}{32}$ of 1% of the systems' assets while the ongoing cost would only amount to $\frac{1}{20}$ of 1% of the assets.

The court agreed with the trustees that pension contracts incorporate common law duties of prudence and loyalty. The trustees failed to show, however, that economically competitive, substitute investments were not available. Moreover, the court accepted the lower court's finding that sufficient investment opportunities remained available to the trustees "to construct an almost perfectly diversified portfolio." The ordinance also contained numerous fail-safe provisions to enable the trustees to avoid significant losses. In addition to a two-year phase-in period, the ordinance allowed the trustees to suspend divestment for 90 days if "they find ... that divestiture has become imprudent." During this time, the trustees can make new investments in companies doing business in South Africa. According to the court, "there exist numerous safeguards which guarantee that divestiture cannot occur unless it would be consistent with the Trustees' duty of prudence."

Without these protections, would the ordinance have impaired the obligation of contract?

†